Forest
Products
Laboratory

General
Technical
Report
FPL–GTR–228

In cooperation
with the

United States
Department of
Transportation

Federal
Highway
Administration

United States Department of Agriculture
Forest Service

Species Identification and Design Value Estimation of Wooden Members in Covered Bridges

Alex C. Wiedenhoeft
David E. Kretschmann

I0411540

Abstract

Covered timber bridges are historic structures with unique aesthetic value. To preserve this value and maintain bridges in service, robust evaluation of their performance and safety is necessary. The strength of the timber found in covered bridges can vary considerably, not only because of age and condition, but also because of species and grade. For the practicing engineer or inspector evaluating a covered bridge, design values for existing wood members must be determined with as much accuracy as possible by accounting for bridge-specific conditions. The current practice is to assign wood values for strength and moduli from existing specifications without specific reference to timber species, condition, or grade, which can result in an inaccurate assessment of the structure. This manual provides a walk-through for basic wood identification, inspection, condition assessment, field grading, and design value estimation for wood in covered bridges.

Keywords: field grading, species identification, covered bridges, inspection, wood anatomy, condition assessment, design value estimation

This study is part of the Research, Technology and Education portion of the **National Historic Covered Bridge Preservation** (NHCBP) Program administered by the Federal Highway Administration. The NHCBP program includes preservation, rehabilitation and restoration of covered bridges that are listed or are eligible for listing on the National Register of Historic Places; research for better means of restoring, and protecting these bridges; development of educational aids; and technology transfer to disseminate information on covered bridges in order to preserve the Nation's cultural heritage.

This study is conducted under a joint agreement between the Federal Highway Administration–Turner Fairbank Highway Research Center, and the Forest Service–Forest Products Laboratory.

Federal Highway Administration Program Manager— Sheila Rimal Duwadi, P.E.

Forest Products Laboratory Program Manager— Michael A. Ritter, P.E.

June 2014

Wiedenhoeft, Alex C.; Kretschmann, David E. 2014. Species identification and design value estimation of wooden members in covered bridges. General Technical Report FPL-GTR-228. Madison, WI: U.S. Department of Agriculture, Forest Service, Forest Products Laboratory. 94 p.

A limited number of free copies of this publication are available to the public from the Forest Products Laboratory, One Gifford Pinchot Drive, Madison, WI 53726–2398. This publication is also available online at www.fpl.fs.fed.us. Laboratory publications are sent to hundreds of libraries in the United States and elsewhere.

The Forest Products Laboratory is maintained in cooperation with the University of Wisconsin.

The use of trade or firm names in this publication is for reader information and does not imply endorsement by the United States Department of Agriculture (USDA) of any product or service.

The USDA prohibits discrimination in all its programs and activities on the basis of race, color, national origin, age, disability, and where applicable, sex, marital status, familial status, parental status, religion, sexual orientation, genetic information, political beliefs, reprisal, or because all or a part of an individual's income is derived from any public assistance program. (Not all prohibited bases apply to all programs.) Persons with disabilities who require alternative means for communication of program information (Braille, large print, audiotape, etc.) should contact USDA's TARGET Center at (202) 720–2600 (voice and TDD). To file a complaint of discrimination, write to USDA, Director, Office of Civil Rights, 1400 Independence Avenue, S.W., Washington, D.C. 20250–9410, or call (800) 795–3272 (voice) or (202) 720–6382 (TDD). USDA is an equal opportunity provider and employer.

Species Identification and Design Value Estimation of Wooden Members in Covered Bridges

Alex C. Wiedenhoeft
David E. Kretschmann

U.S. Department of Agriculture ▪ Forest Service ▪ Forest Products Laboratory

Contents

Species Identification and Design Value Estimation of Wooden Members in Covered Bridges

Alex C. Wiedenhoeft, Research Botanist
David E. Kretschmann, Research General Engineer
Forest Products Laboratory, Madison, Wisconsin

Introduction

To extend the service life of historic covered bridges in the United States, methods for accurately estimating the strength and safety of the wooden structural members are necessary. In the absence of dynamic loading or other experimental load assessment data, performance estimates must be based on the specific details of a bridge's construction. There are three critical steps needed to make a useful estimate: (1) determine the woods used, (2) estimate the grade of wood used, and (3) assess the condition of the timber being graded. With accurate information, an engineer or other professional can make determinations about maintenance, repair, restoration, or decommissioning the structure. If accurate information is not available, historic bridges may be prematurely replaced. Engaging a skilled and experienced inspector familiar with wood identification, timber grading, and condition assessment is best, but that is not always possible. This field guide describes the most critical considerations when examining a historic covered bridge and can empower an inspector to make an informed judgment about the need for further, detailed analysis of the bridge in question.

Background

When a new wooden bridge is constructed, a structural engineer relies on the current design values for a known species and the local building codes to determine the appropriate size and grade of timber required for particular service loads. The strength of timber found in historic covered bridges can vary considerably because of age and condition. Uncertainty can also be introduced when estimating strength of members if the species and grade are unknown. Most historic wooden bridges were constructed before standardized grading practices for timbers were agreed upon. For evaluation purposes, design value estimates for existing wood members must be assigned with as much accuracy as possible. This is impossible when the type, grade, and condition of the existing wood are uncertain. The current practice for wood in service in historical structures is to assign values for strength and moduli from existing specifications based on assumed species and grade, but often these assumptions are inaccurate for the specific conditions and can result in an unreliable assessment of the structure. An inspection should determine the species, evaluate the condition of the member, and determine an estimate of the grade before estimating the capacity of the members and thus allow for the estimation of the safe loading conditions for the bridge. This evaluation process is complicated, and even with the best available information, can require considerable engineering judgment.

Objective and scope of the manual

The objective of this publication is to provide a field inspection manual for covered bridge inspection engineers that addresses the topics of wood identification, grading, condition assessment, and a possible method of design value estimation for wood members used in covered timber bridges.

The continued use of covered bridges is dependent on an affirmation that they meet appropriate strength thresholds given their intended use. Because this directly affects public safety, every step in the process of making a design value estimate must be performed with care, precision, and a robust understanding of the factors that affect it. For this reason, this manual addresses each step of the process that leads to a design value estimate—wood species identification, member grading, on-site condition assessment, and calculating an appropriate strength—with a high degree of detail. It is intended for use by professionals who, though lacking the formal background in wood science, are committed to mastering the skills and information necessary to arrive at a reliable result. Each section presents the level of detail needed to make a valid estimate. The content will also empower the user to make a judgment about the advisability of securing the services of a consulting engineer—if the reader is comfortable with using it, this manual provides the user with what is needed. If a consulting engineer is needed, the reader will be able to more easily communicate with them about the problems and concerns found in the bridge.

1 | Wood identification and pattern recognition

Wood identification is a combination of art and science. Whereas the bulk of the wood identification section of this manual focuses on the scientific characteristics used to make accurate field identifications of wood, the contribution of the artistic component to the identification process should be neither overlooked nor understated. There is nothing specific you must do to train yourself in the artistic aspects of wood identification; your mind will do this automatically. The scientific aspects, on the other hand, are not as easy as the artistic portion of the process and will come only with diligent study, practice, and focus.

Wood identification is a process of pattern recognition. The patterns you will learn to recognize are patterns of wood structure; that is, specific cells in specific arrangements, many of which have specific terminology associated with them. At first the terminology may be daunting, but with practice the terms will take on meaning.

The process of identifying a wood specimen is a microcosm of the process of learning to identify any object. It is very similar to learning to identify anything—wood, birds, chairs, people. All these identifications are governed by the same processes of cognition resulting in recognition of a pattern (Figs. 1.1, 1.2). Identification begins with careful observation, proceeds to mental comparison with similar woods, and then makes reference to a formal means of confirming an identification (e.g., reference to images in this manual or a small collection of correctly identified specimens).

To be able to gather information about the characters in a piece of wood, you must understand the basic biology of wood; use the correct tools; be able to prepare the wood for observation; and make careful observations of wood characters. These characters are employed in an identification key, and then from the key the user is directed to species pages that provide more detailed information for confirming an identification.

Before the topics of using a hand lens, preparing wood for observation, and understanding the characters used in wood identification can be tackled, a general introduction to the biology of wood is needed. The discussion of wood biology is restricted to trees here, though much of what is presented is also true of shrubs and lianas.

The treatments of wood structure and wood identification in this manual are fairly rigorous and will provide the foundation necessary to identify not just the common woods found in North American covered bridges but also tropical woods, though the latter are not dealt with in the identification key presented here. Additional references for wood identification are presented in Chapter 8, so if you wish to extend your knowledge of wood identification, the fundamentals in this manual will set you on a firm path.

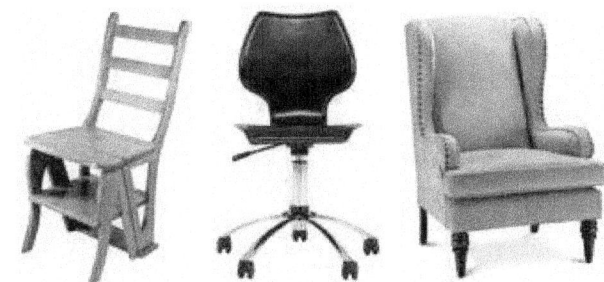

Figure 1.1—We use pattern recognition in all aspects of our daily lives. All three of these objects are chairs, despite the differences in materials and design.

Figure 1.2—The process of learning to distinguish identical twins is similar to the process of learning to identify wood.

2 | Basic wood biology—anatomy for identification

It is not a simple matter to organize the gross structure and biology of wood into an easy-to-understand text. It may be necessary to move back and forth between some concepts in this chapter in an effort to present a unified concept of wood structure for wood identification. Some sections of this chapter will be difficult to understand fully the first time through; read it a second time after thinking about the material, and the once-unfamiliar concepts will be clearer. Keep in mind that in addition to permitting us to identify wood, the cells and their characteristics give wood its physical and mechanical properties such as stiffness. Other features of timber that influence strength and performance, such as knots, are also biologically derived. The condition of a timber is often affected by external biological agents such as decay fungi or insects, and the ability of a timber to resist such attack is likewise founded on the biology of the tree from which the wood came. The distance between the details of the anatomical structure of wood and the ultimate determination of the load capacity of a timber bridge is not as great as it might seem at first.

2.1 Wood as a cellular material

Wood, like all living or once-living materials, is made from millions and millions of interconnected cells that form a larger structure, in much the same way your heart or liver is made of many different cells. Cells are the basic building blocks of larger organisms, and most of the identification sections of this manual focus on understanding different types, shapes, orientations, and groups of cells in wood.

2.2 Two systems of cells in wood

Wood is made of two interlocking systems of cells, the axial system and the radial system (Fig. 2.1). The axial system is all the cells running up and down the trunk of the tree or along the grain of a board. The radial system is made up of rays, groups of cells running from the center of the tree out toward the bark. Rays and the radial system in general are less familiar to the casual observer of wood but are critical to understanding and identifying wood. Because tree trunks are generally round, the cells in the axial system are lined up in overlapping, curved layers.

2.3 Heartwood, sapwood, and pith

When looking at a cut stump or a disc from a tree (Fig. 2.2), there are two basic domains in most woods: the central typically darkly colored (and sometimes odiferous) area called heartwood, and the typically lighter colored outer strip of wood under the bark, the sapwood. There is no appreciable structural difference between heartwood and sapwood; the difference is one of accumulated biochemicals in the heartwood. The center of the tree is called the pith; this is the tissue formed before the first wood is made by the tree.

2.4 Growth rings

Wood is formed of discrete layers called growth rings. They represent the basic building blocks of wood structure that span the microscopic, cellular nature of wood and that which can be seen with the naked eye (Fig. 2.3). A growth ring is all the wood formed during one period of growth,

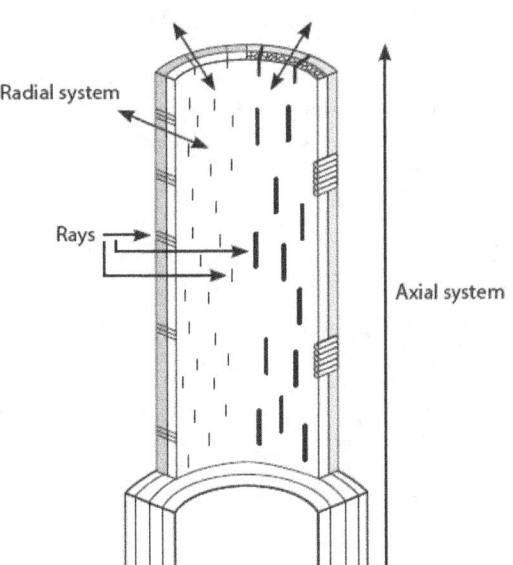

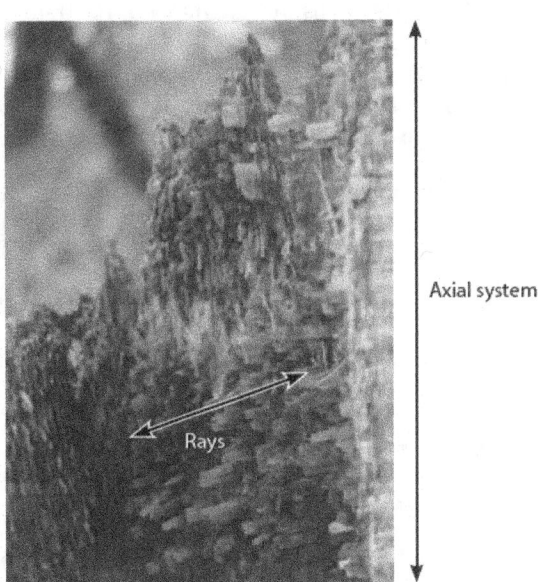

Figure 2.1—Axial and radial systems in wood. The diagram on the left shows a simplification of the axial and radial systems. The photograph on the right shows a decayed stump in which much of the axial system has been removed by fungi. The card-like tabs protruding are the rays of the radial system.

for our purposes one year, that can be distinguished by some anatomical characteristic from the wood formed during a different growth period. When you look at the end grain of a board or the cut end of a log or a stump, the concentric circles you can see are most likely growth rings. The portion of a growth ring formed at the beginning of the growing season is known as earlywood, and it is found closer to the pith. The portion of the growth ring formed later in the season is called latewood, and it is found toward the outside of the tree (this is discussed in greater detail in Chapter 5). The rays of the radial system appear as lines perpendicular to the growth rings when the end grain of a board or a stump is examined.

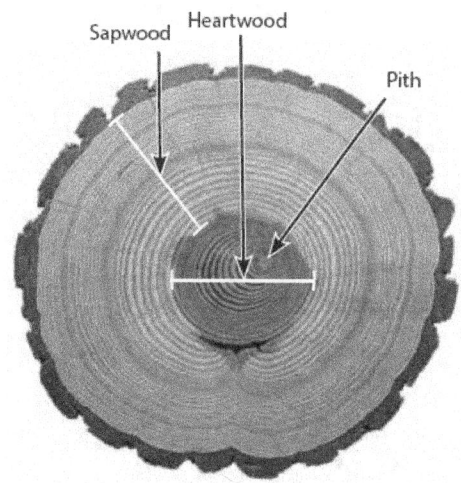

Figure 2.2—The end grain of a log. Bark surrounds the log. Inside this is the wood. The light colored wood is sapwood, the dark colored wood is heartwood. The small dot representing the center of the tree is the pith.

2.5 The planes of section

The relationship between the cells of the axial system and the rays of the radial system, the round shape of a tree trunk, and the concentric nature of growth rings around the trunk combine to give us three primary ways to view a piece of wood. These three views are known as planes of section, and understanding them is one of the most difficult aspects of, but also absolutely necessary for, wood identification.

There are two fundamental ways to cut wood: across the grain and along the grain. When we cut wood, whether to view it with a hand lens or to produce a board, the easiest cut to understand is across the grain. This is the transverse cut that loggers make when they fell a tree. This cut is perpendicular to the trunk and thus across the grain of the wood—across the axial system (Fig. 2.4). The surface you see once this cut is made is the transverse plane of section

or transverse surface, also known as the end-grain of the wood. On the transverse surface we can see the curving nature of the growth rings and the way in which the rays of the radial system run perpendicular to that curvature; the rays appear as straight lines running from the center of the tree out toward the bark. To understand the other two planes of section, we must understand this relationship between rays, growth rings, and the round form of a tree trunk.

The second fundamental way to cut wood is along the grain; doing this produces a longitudinal cut and exposes a longitudinal surface. Although it is possible to cut along the grain in any orientation with respect to the rays and growth rings, the structure of wood shows us that there are two basic ways to cut it, either parallel to the rays, or perpendicular to them. Because the rays and growth rings are perpendicular to each other, we can cut perpendicular to the growth rings, or parallel to them. Not all woods, however, have obvious growth rings, so we will orient ourselves by speaking of the cut in reference to the orientation of the rays.

When we cut along the grain and parallel to the rays, we produce a radial surface or radial plane of section. This exposes the rays like lines running across the surface and is little used in the hand lens identification of wood. If a round piece of firewood is split exactly in half, from one side to the other through the center of the tree, the flat surface is a radial surface.

The longitudinal cut perpendicular to the rays is the tangential plane of section, or tangential surface. This exposes the cut ends of the rays and allows us to understand the size,

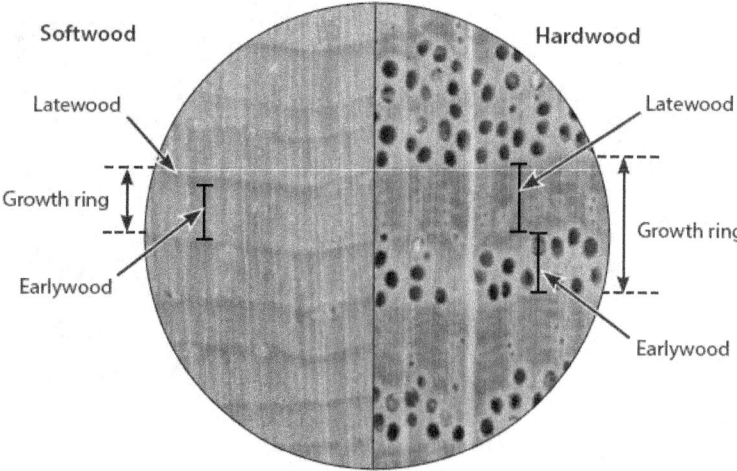

Figure 2.3—Growth rings in a softwood and a hardwood. Although the structure of these two woods is quite distinct, both have growth rings and the growth rings can be divided into earlywood and latewood.

spacing, and arrangement of the rays. This is the view of wood we would have if we could walk up to a standing tree and tear away the bark to view the wood.

We can use two analogies to clarify these ideas: geometry and apple pie (Fig. 2.4). In the geometry example, we draw a circle. Any line from the center of the circle to the edge of the circle is a radius of that circle. The radius in geometry is the ray in wood (and indeed in the source of the name term "ray"). A line that touches a circle at one point is called a tangent line, and any radius of a circle that intersects with a tangent line is perpendicular to it at that point, and parallel to the edge of the circle at that point. The edge of the circle represents a growth ring, the radius a ray, and thus if we are perpendicular to the ray, we are parallel to the growth ring. By extending this two-dimensional circle geometry to a three-dimensional cylinder and extending either the radius or the tangent line up and down the cylinder, we produce a radial or tangential plane of section, respectively.

The second analogy is more accessible. If we start with a freshly baked, delicious apple pie, we have a round object. When we cut the pie to share it with our family, we make cuts from the edge of the pie into and across the center until we have a number of wedge-shaped pie pieces. Each pie piece shows all three planes of section. The top and bottom crusts of the pie are the transverse surfaces. The exposed apple filling along the two cut edges are radial surfaces, and the outer, curved portion of crust that was against the pie pan is a curving tangential surface.

We identify people we know mostly by facial characteristics. Hand-lens wood identification uses primarily features on the transverse surface, thus it can be said to be the "face" of wood. For this reason, any reference to the appearance of a character will be on the transverse surface unless otherwise stated. We will do little or nothing with the radial or tangential surfaces. One way to perfect your understanding is to make careful three-dimensional drawings of the relations between the planes of section without looking at the figures. When you can explain the planes of section to someone else, your understanding of planes of section is complete.

2.6 Softwoods and hardwoods

The topics we have covered thus far in this chapter are true of all woods in the manual, regardless of species or origin. The remainder of the chapter is devoted to drawing some fundamental distinctions between different kinds of woods and understanding the anatomical and cellular bases for their differences.

There are two fundamental types of wood: softwoods and hardwoods (Fig. 2.5). Softwoods come from needle-leaved and cone-bearing trees like pines, spruces, firs, and cedars. Hardwoods come from broad-leaved and flower-bearing trees like walnut, oak, ash, and elm. The distinction between hardwoods and softwoods is thus a botanical one, and in the forest can most easily be seen by differences in external characteristics like leaf shape, the nature of the reproductive structures (cones vs. flowers), and the architecture of the tree itself. In addition to these external features, the cells that comprise the wood of softwoods and hardwoods are quite different structurally. Thus, hardwoods and softwoods are easily distinguishable from each other in the process of wood

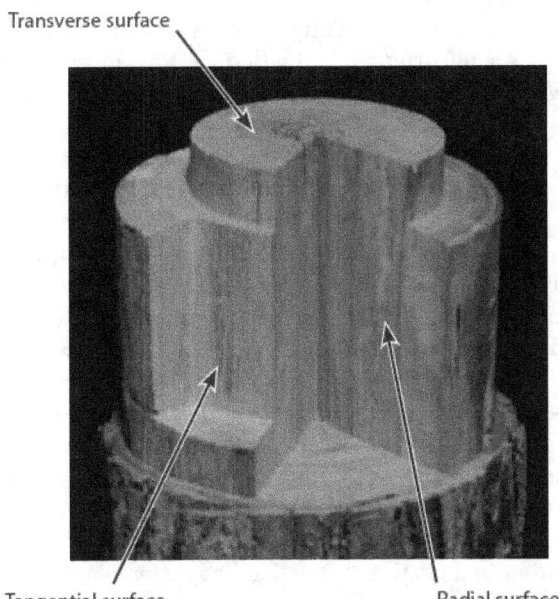

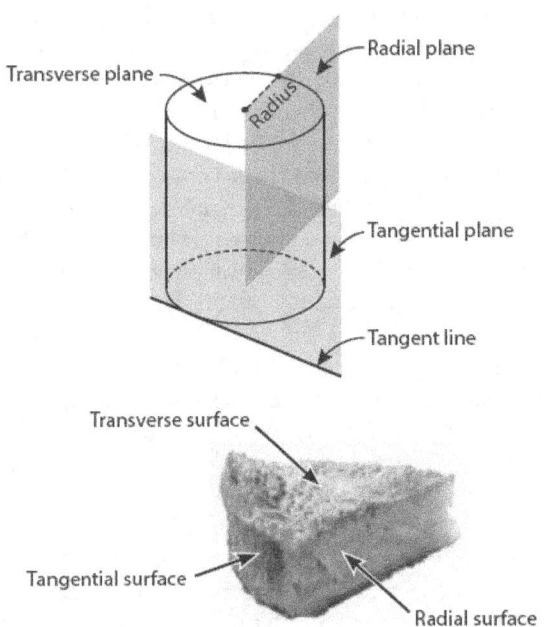

Figure 2.4—The planes of section illustrated three different ways. On the left is a photograph of a small log that has been cut across the grain to expose the transverse surface and cut along to grain to expose the radial and tangential surfaces. On the upper right is an illustration showing the relationship between radial and tangential planes in a simple cylinder. On the bottom right, a piece of apple pie shows the three planes of section. The top and bottom of the piece of pie represent transverse surfaces and the cut sides represent radial surfaces. The curved outer crust of the pie represents the tangential surface.

Figure 2.5—Two examples of the transverse surface of softwoods and two examples of hardwoods. On the left, top and bottom, are two softwoods, as well as a silhouette of a generic softwood tree. On the right, top and bottom, are two hardwoods, as well as a generic hardwood silhouette.

identification. Though softwoods and hardwoods are structurally distinct (as will be explained in detail below) both are still wood. They have axial and radial systems, heartwood and sapwood, growth rings, and can be cut to produce transverse, radial, and tangential planes of section. Cells in wood are either dead at functional maturity (one type of cell in softwoods, two types of cells in hardwoods) or are alive at functional maturity. In both softwoods and hardwoods, these living cells are called parenchyma cells. Parenchyma cells can be a part of the axial system of both softwoods and hardwoods, and make up virtually all the cells in the radial system (that is, rays are composed of parenchyma cells).

2.7 The specific cellular anatomy of softwoods

The cellular anatomy of softwoods is simple compared to that of hardwoods (Fig. 2.6). The axial system is formed predominantly of one kind of cell, the tracheid. With a hand lens, tracheids appear as small boxes or rectangles. In species with obvious growth rings, the earlywood tracheids are typically thin-walled and the open spaces in the cells, the lumina, can be seen as dark centers. In such species, the cell walls of the latewood are much thicker, and often the lumina of the cells cannot be seen. The second and less prevalent cell type in the axial system of softwoods is axial parenchyma, either as scattered solitary cells, or forming special structures called resin canals. Resin canals are discussed later as an important character for the identification of

softwoods. The radial system, as in all woods, is composed of ray parenchyma cells. It is not possible to see individual softwood ray parenchyma cells with a hand lens, but the rays they compose are faintly visible as straight lines running perpendicular to the growth rings. Rays in softwoods are generally only one cell wide, and this is why they appear only faintly.

2.8 The specific cellular anatomy of hardwoods

The cellular wood anatomy of hardwoods is more complex than that of softwoods (Fig. 2.6) because there are three main cell types in the axial system: vessels, axial parenchyma, and fibers. Vessels are the characteristic cell type of hardwoods; all hardwoods in the manual have vessels, and no softwoods in the manual have them. Thus, the presence of vessels is definitive proof that a wood is a hardwood. Vessels are dead cells specialized for water conduction and are generally much larger and rounder than tracheids in softwoods. They appear as round pipes or holes in the wood, and understanding the variation in their structure, size, distribution, and relative proportions is a major component of hardwood identification.

Axial parenchyma cells in hardwoods are, as with all parenchyma cells, living cells when functioning in the tree. Axial parenchyma in hardwoods is much more common, and its distribution much more complex, than in softwoods. Axial parenchyma is generally only visible with a hand lens

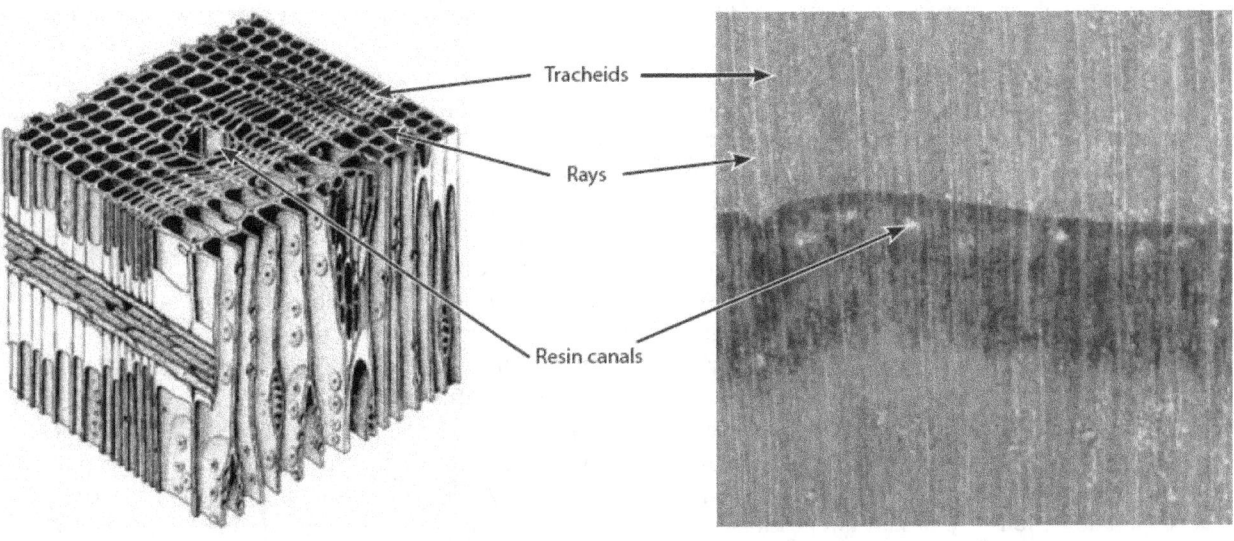

Softwoods

Tracheids

Rays

Resin canals

Hardwoods

Vessels

Rays

Fibers

Figure 2.6—Anatomical differences between softwoods (top) and hardwoods (bottom). Softwoods are composed mostly of tracheids, which can be thin-walled in the earlywood and thick-walled in the latewood, and rays running vertically in the image on the right. The illustration on the left shows more detail and is drawn at a higher magnification than the hand-lens view of the transverse surface of a softwood on the right. Shown in both images are resin canals. Hardwoods are structurally more complex than softwoods, with vessels, fibers, axial parenchyma, and rays. The vessels are the dark holes scattered throughout the wood. The rays are the lines running vertically in the image. The axial parenchyma in this wood appears as light-colored, round halos around the vessels. The individual fibers are too small to be seen, but together form the brown tissue in which the other cells are embedded. As with the softwood above, the illustration on the left is presented at a higher magnification than the hand-lens view of the transverse surface on the right. Note that in this hardwood, there is no clear distinction between earlywood and latewood. This is discussed in more detail in Chapter 5.

when it occurs in groups of many parenchyma cells. It is generally seen as a lighter colored tissue compared to the other cells in the wood. Hardwoods present a great range of axial parenchyma patterns and abundance, ranging from barely visible with a microscope to easily seen with the naked eye. Along with variations in vessel characteristics, the amount, distribution, and type of axial parenchyma present in a wood is one of the major sets of characters used in hardwood identification.

Fibers are dead, thick-walled cells and are not usually individually visible with a hand lens, but in any given hardwood, groups of fibers usually form a large percentage of the visible cells. Though it is an awkward way to describe their appearance, fibers are most easily seen and understood by subtraction; if you are looking at cells of the axial system that are not vessels or axial parenchyma, they are fibers.

The radial system of hardwoods is composed of ray parenchyma, and like softwoods, it is usually not possible to discern individual ray parenchyma cells. Unlike softwoods, hardwoods have a tremendous variety of ray widths, ranging from rays one cell wide and barely visible (as in softwoods) to rays more than 60 cells wide, and easily seen at a distance with the naked eye.

2.9 Understanding scientific names

From this point forward, this manual refers to woods using the trade names listed in the National Design Specification (NDS) Supplement *Design Values for Wood Construction* (AWC 2012). The use of a standardized list for American woods simplifies the use of this manual in conjunction with the NDS Supplement. Ultimately, however, the NDS Supplement trade names refer back to woods whose official names are scientific names.

Scientific names are made of two words, a genus name and a specific epithet. Both the genus and the specific epithet are italicized or underlined when printed. The genus name is the first word of the two and is always capitalized. The specific epithet is the second word of the two and is not capitalized. In scientific names, the genus name (or genus) is like a surname; it designates to the group to which the species most closely belongs. The specific epithet is like a given name (first name), distinguishing that species from all others in the genus.

For ponderosa pine, the scientific name is *Pinus ponderosa.* The word *Pinus* is the genus name, and the word *ponderosa* is the specific epithet. There are many other species in the genus *Pinus,* including *P. taeda* (loblolly pine), and *P. strobus* (eastern white pine). Note that the genus was abbreviated by placing a period after the first letter and omitting the rest of the word. This is done only after the genus has been spelled out already, and is a convention that saves space. Note also that it did not say "There are many other species in the genus *Pinus* including, *taeda* and *strobus.*" Although it would have been clear that the subject was a species of *Pinus,* in other cases such a shortcut might lead to confusion in much the same way using only a given name,

John, is not specific enough to distinguish him from all the other people with that given name. If his surname were a common name such as Smith, there would likely be hundreds or thousands of other people named John Smith in the world. Such confusion is prevented in scientific names by a simple rule; the same combination of genus name and specific epithet may not be used to refer to more than one species. Thus, there is only one *Pinus ponderosa* in the world, and its scientific name can never be confused with that of any other species.

Learning to use scientific names correctly empowers you to communicate precisely. Sometimes the group to which a wood belongs is between the level of species and genus. This is common in genera (the plural of genus) with many species, or in genera where the wood of different species is dramatically different. For example, the genus *Pinus* has many species scatted across the northern hemisphere and different groups of species have different anatomical characteristics. For example, *Pinus taeda* is a species that belongs to the yellow pine group, and so its identity would be reported as *Pinus* sp., yellow pine group, because though it can be determined that it is not a member of the red pine group, the exact species within the yellow pine group cannot be determined. There is no special or convenient scientific word to use, so the scientific name is combined with additional information written in plain language to indicate the proper level of specificity in the identification.

3 | Correct use of a hand lens

Fig. 3.1—A hand lens has two main parts, the lens and the housing.

A hand lens is a powerful tool for the identification of wood, but like all tools it must be used correctly to take full advantage of its powers. The hand lens has two main parts (Fig. 3.1), a lens that magnifies the object of interest (generally we use 10× or 14× lenses in wood identification; a 14× lens is recommended for use with this manual) and a housing to hold and protect the lens. Unlike a microscope that is able to focus at different distances depending on the specimen and the configuration of the various lenses, thus requiring much adjusting, a hand lens has a fixed focal length. There is only one distance between the lens and the object that will produce a sharp image. This distance is easily found by examining a coin or other familiar object with the lens, but is generally only 1–4 cm between the lens and the specimen. Most hand lenses have no "front" or "back" to them; you can look through either side of the lens at a specimen.

Because there is only one distance between the lens and the object that will produce a good image, the remaining variable is the distance between the lens and your eye. For the best results, the hand lens should be placed as close to your eye as possible (Fig. 3.2); it is common for your eyelashes to brush against the lens when it is used correctly. Many people find this unnatural at first, but it is essential that this close distance be used. Before trying to look at a specimen of wood, use the lens to examine common objects: the cloth of a shirt, the print in this manual, a fingernail, or other things of interest. Force yourself to keep the lens close to your eye, and practice adjusting the distance between the lens and the object. At first, it will probably be helpful to close your other eye, but after a few minutes of examining common objects, practice using the lens with both eyes open. Although this can be difficult for many people, it is a good skill to practice because it will reduce eye strain.

It can be difficult to ensure that enough light reaches the specimen when using a hand lens; your hands and head will block light and shade the specimen (Fig. 3.3), making it hard to observe details. It is tempting to move the lens away from your eye at this point so that more light falls on the object. Do not do this. Instead, you must reorient your body so that light falls on the specimen. Sometimes this process of finding sufficient lighting requires you to turn to a different angle, bend at the waist, or take other action to find ample light. If you are identifying wood in the field, it may be necessary to remove a small specimen and move out from the shade of the structure into the direct sunlight. Although this may seem like a minor point, taking pains to secure good lighting has several benefits. First, it allows the hand lens to perform to its full capacity as a tool. Second, it ensures that the object, ultimately an unknown wood specimen, can be observed in sufficient detail to permit identification. Last, it reduces eye strain, allowing you to gain more experience and practice wood identification more comfortably.

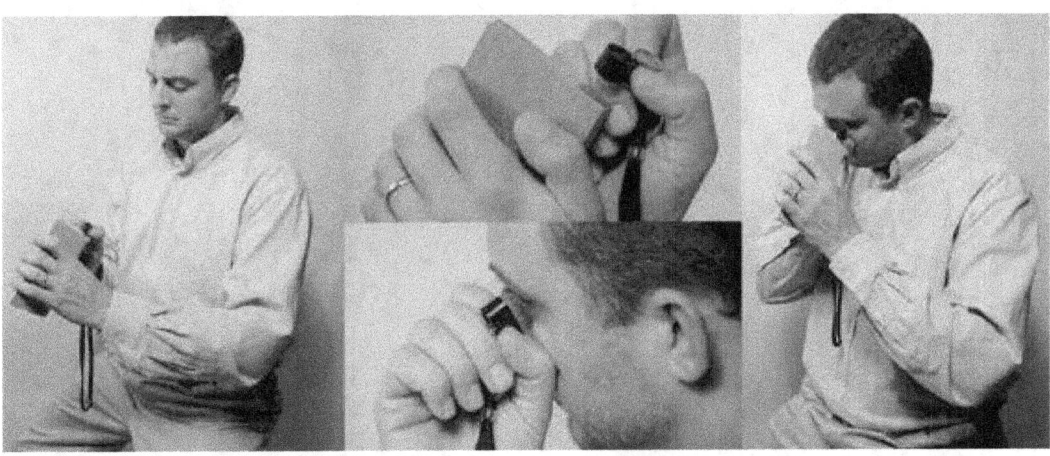

Figure 3.2—Using a hand lens to observe a wood specimen. On the left, the distance between the lens and the observer's eye is much too great, but the distance between the lens and wood specimen is correct. The top photo in the center shows the correct distance between the lens and the wood specimen. The bottom photo in the center shows the correct distance between the lens and the eye. The photograph on the right shows the correct distances between the lens, the specimen, and the eye.

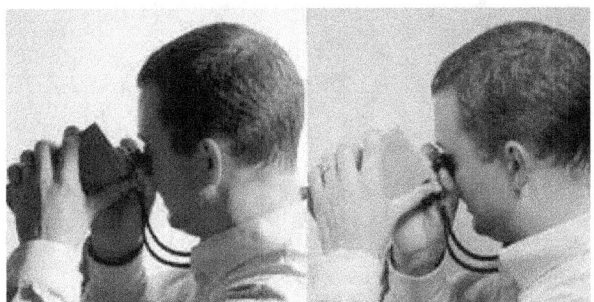

Figure 3.3—On the left, the observer's head is blocking the light, and the specimen cannot be observed properly. On the right, the observer is allowing light to fall on the specimen to ensure accurate observation.

4 | Wood specimen preparation for hand lens observation

The single most difficult physical skill involved in wood identification is producing a smoothly prepared surface for observing anatomical features. This skill must be practiced patiently; it takes time to become proficient at this task. Producing a cleanly cut surface is also the only appreciably dangerous aspect of wood identification with a hand lens; the tools used to cut the wood are necessarily sharp, and injuries from minor cuts to major lacerations can result from carelessness, fatigue, or poor technique. Safety must always be the first priority, followed closely by the secondary importance of making a serviceable cut of the wood. Because this skill is both necessary and inherently dangerous, patience and prudence must be exercised while learning. Before trying to cut a specimen of wood with these techniques, please read and understand this entire chapter.

4.1 The principles of cutting
A few basic principles apply to cutting any material, and you are likely already familiar with them from everyday experience. The first and most important principle is the idea of drawing the edge of your cutting tool across the surface you intend to cut. One of the easiest ways to think about this is in terms of slicing a tomato (Fig. 4.1): if you try to push the edge of a knife straight through the tomato, even the sharpest knife will crush the tomato rather than make a

nice slice (Fig. 4.1a). If you saw back and forth many times with the knife edge as you slice the tomato, you produce ragged and uneven slices (Fig. 4.1b,c). The best technique is to draw the edge of the knife a single time through the tomato as the downward motion is applied (Fig. 4.1d). This gives you the maximum cutting ability of the edge of the knife and produces clean, even slices (Fig. 4.1e). If I place the edge of the same knife on my thumb with slight pressure, it does not cut me (Fig. 4.1f). If I slide the edge of the knife along my thumb under the same pressure, I will be cut. When we cut wood to view it with a hand lens, we must draw the edge of the cutting tool across the area we are preparing; no other technique will suffice.

A second principle of cutting has to do with the relationships between the blade and the material to be cut. Harder materials generally require a steeper cutting angle than softer materials (Fig. 4.2). Harder materials generally require sturdier blades to cut them as well. For example, you can shave hair with a thin razor, but to cut copper wire, you will use much thicker wire cutters. To prepare wood for observation with a hand lens, we will use the utility knife (Fig. 4.3). The harder the wood, the steeper the cutting angle, and the softer the wood, the shallower the angle. For woods in covered bridges, the utility knife is the necessary tool.

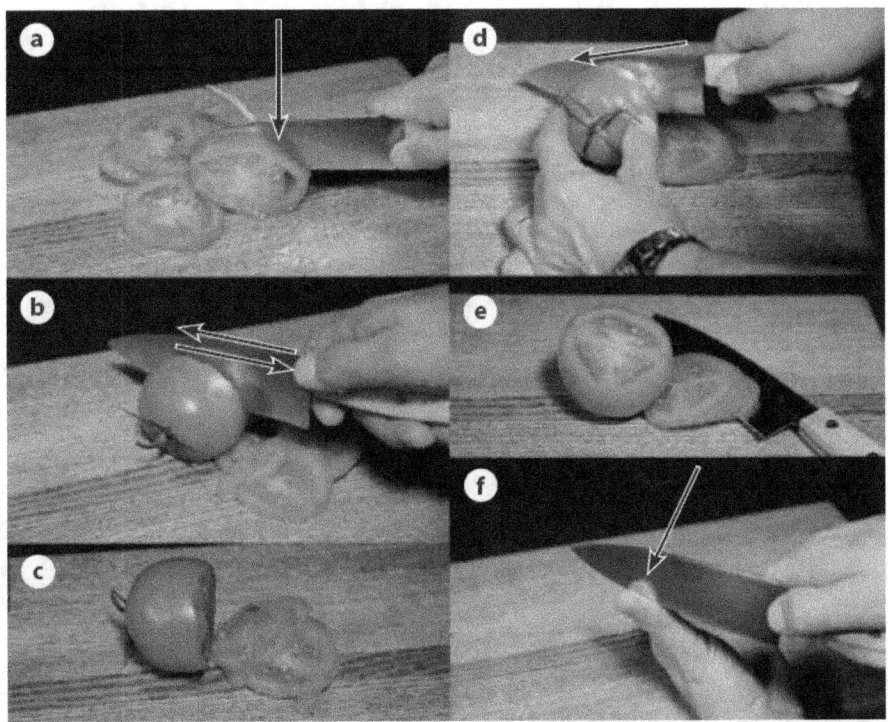

Figure 4.1—Slicing a tomato illustrates the principles of cutting wood: (a) Pushing a sharp knife downward through a tomato crushes it. (b) Sawing back and forth through the tomato makes uneven slices (c). (d) Passing the knife through the tomato with one even stroke maximizes the cutting ability of the blade and produces clean slices (e). (f) Pushing the blade into the thumb does not cut the skin.

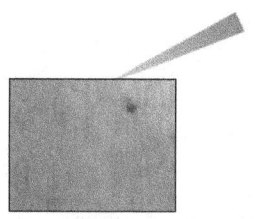
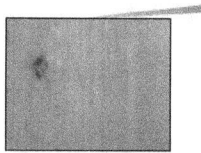

Figure 4.2—Illustrations of cutting angles for hard, dense woods and softer woods. On the left, the angle of the knife to the wood is high because the wood is dense, and the thicker blade is needed. On the right, the angle of the knife is low because the wood is light and soft, and the thinner, sharper blade is needed.

Figure 4.3—The preferred basic tool for cutting wood, utility knives will make clean cuts of all but the softest woods.

4.2 Holding the knife

To cut wood safely and effectively, it is necessary to hold the knife correctly. The safest and most powerful method of cutting wood might contradict what you have been told about using a knife. Most people are taught to cut away from themselves, to minimize the chances of a laceration. For surfacing wood specimens, you will cut toward yourself, but you will do it in a controlled and failsafe way that, if done correctly, makes it impossible to cut yourself. This is accomplished by using the correct knife grip (Fig. 4.4). Begin with an open hand, thumb extended, fingers held loosely together. Lay the knife in the palm of your hand such that the base of the blade (where it joins the handle) is close to but not in contact with the web of skin between your thumb and index finger, with the edge of the blade facing your thumb (Fig. 4.4a,b). If the edge is extended too far from your hand, you will lose the force needed to make a good cut (Fig. 4.4c); if the edge of the blade is touching your skin, you will cut yourself badly (Fig. 4.4d) Now, taking care that the knife does not shift either closer to or farther from the web of skin between the index finger and the thumb,

close your fingers firmly over the handle of the knife. Wrap your thumb loosely over your fingers. This is the basic grip. When it is time to cut a specimen, you will use your thumb as a fulcrum to pull the knife through the specimen by closing your fist tightly.

▸ DO NOT try to cut a wood specimen yet.

4.3 Holding the specimen

With the knife occupying your dominant hand, your other hand must hold the specimen. There are two simple rules for holding the specimen. First, you must grip the specimen quite firmly, as it takes considerable force to produce a cleanly cut surface on a wood specimen. Too loose a grip, and the specimen will sail from your grasp and you might cut yourself. Second, keep all parts of your hand away from the path of the blade; do not in any way hold the specimen near the area you intend to cut (Fig. 4.5). All body parts must be well away from the cutting area or shielded on the leeward side of the specimen to have a safe and effective grasp on the specimen.

▸ DO NOT try to cut a wood specimen yet.

4.4 Choosing a specimen

When working in the field, you will likely not have much control over the size and shape of wood specimen you must identify, but when you are practicing these techniques, wise choice of specimens is critical. Select a specimen that is approximately the length and width of your hand. The thickness of the specimen should be between 1 and 3 cm; any thinner and it may flex or break, any thicker and it will be difficult to hold firmly.

▸ DO NOT try to cut a wood specimen yet.

4.5 Orienting the specimen

In addition to questions of knife angle outlined in the section on the principles of cutting, you must also orient the edge of the knife relative to the specimen to produce a precise plane of section. If you are cutting a transverse surface, the edge of the knife must cut through the specimen perpendicular to the axial system, not merely perpendicular to

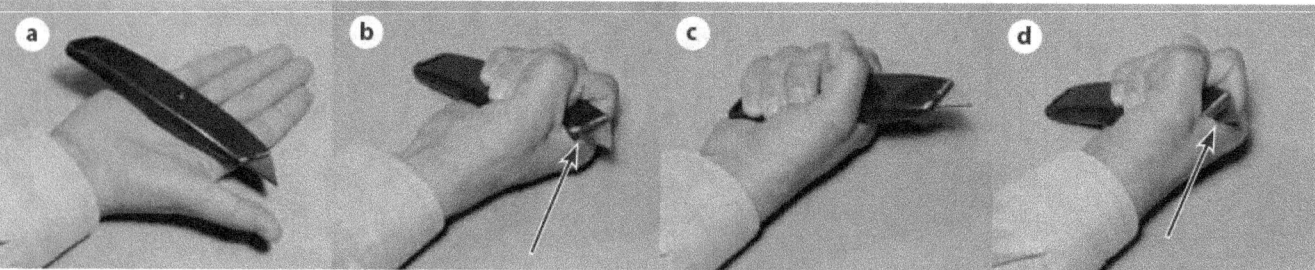

Figure 4.4—Holding the utility knife safely. (a) Begin with an open hand, and orient the utility knife as shown. (b) Close the fingers and wrap the thumb over the fingers; this is the basic grip. Note that the base of the blade is not touching the web of skin between the index finger and the thumb (arrow). (c) The distance between the blade and the hand is much too large and it will be difficult to have the strength to make a clean cut of a wood specimen. (d) The blade of the knife is in contact with the skin between the index finger and the thumb (arrow), and will cut the skin.

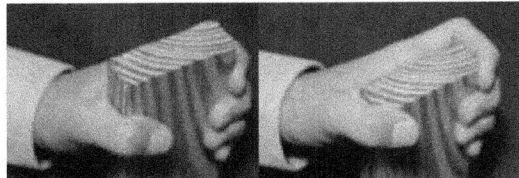

Figure 4.5—The correct grip for holding a specimen for cutting (left). Note that the fingers and thumb are below the top of the specimen and will not be cut. On the right, the specimen is held with the fingers and thumbs in a way that will result in injury when the specimen is cut.

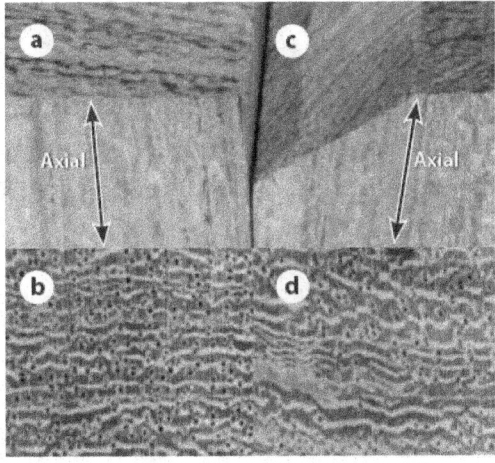

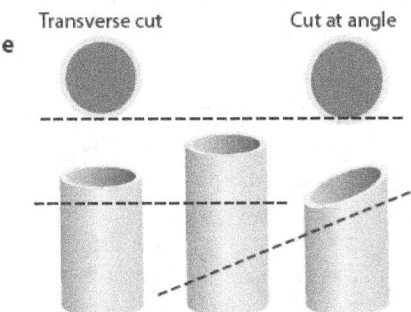

Figure 4.6—When cutting a transverse surface for observation with a hand lens, the cut must be oriented relative to the cells of the axial system, not relative to the surface of specimen (a). A good cut is perpendicular to the axial system and produces a surface in which the anatomical features appear normal (b). Cutting at an angle to the axial system produces a surface in which the anatomical features appear stretched (d). A perpendicular (left) and angled (right) cut through a pipe (e). The perpendicular cut produces an accurate representation of the circular shape of the pipe, whereas the angled cut produces an oval representation.

the surface of the specimen (Fig. 4.6a,b); if you are out of plane by more than one or two degrees, the anatomy of the wood will take a stretched appearance and not be interpretable (Fig. 4.6c,d). Likewise, if you are making a tangential surface, the edge of the knife must be perpendicular to the rays as seen on the transverse surface, and the edge must cut evenly along (and not across at an angle) the grain. In either case, careful orientation of the specimen and the knife is critical.

Consider a section of plastic pipe: if you make a true transverse cut through the pipe, the end of the pipe will appear as a perfect circle, but if you cut at some angle through the pipe, the opening in the end of the pipe will be elliptical (Fig. 4.6e). Because the cells in wood are essentially tiny pipes, the orientation of the knife edge relative to the structure of the wood is critical.

It is important to note that your job is to orient the knife edge relative to the direction of the cells in the wood, not relative to the cut surfaces of your block. It is common for wood specimens to be cut imperfectly; what appears with your naked eye as a transverse surface may in fact be 5 or 10 degrees out of plane.

▶ DO NOT try to cut a wood specimen yet.

4.6 Making the cut

If you have followed the critical directions for holding the knife and the specimen, you now need only be mindful of the position of your thumb on the knife hand. It should be pressed to the near side of the wood specimen, well below the top of the specimen so that it is physically impossible for you to slip and cut yourself. Review the instructions for holding the knife and the comments about the primacy of safety before continuing.

You now have a knife, a wood specimen, an initial sense of what you are trying to accomplish, and know where to put your fingers so that you end the day with as many as you began it. The next question is where on the block should you cut? Because you are using your thumb as a fulcrum for the cutting motion and protecting it away from the path of the knife, the best way to maximize the force in your cut is to cut the corner nearest your thumb. This is true for all three planes of section. By keeping the blade closer to your thumb, your hand doesn't need to stretch far and you can have maximum leverage. To cut, you draw the edge of the

knife through the wood, starting your cut with the base of the blade at the farthest point from your thumb, and pulling the knife toward your hand by firmly making a fist (Fig. 4.7). The exposed portion of a utility knife blade is approximately 2 cm long, so your total cutting motion as you draw the knife through the wood will only be maybe 3–4 cm in length, because of the angle of the blade and the way you pull it though the specimen. This is not a large motion, and it should be done smoothly and confidently. You will make a comparatively small surface, especially at first. This is acceptable because the surface is meant to be viewed with your hand lens, and this will make the area seem much larger.

The first few times you try this you will almost certainly fail. As long as your failure does not involve blood, it is actually a success, as failure is a part of the learning process. If your knife angle is too steep, the blade will bury in the specimen. If it is too shallow, the edge of the knife will not bite into the wood. Practice thoughtfully, rereading the chapter as needed to understand what went wrong. If the edge of the

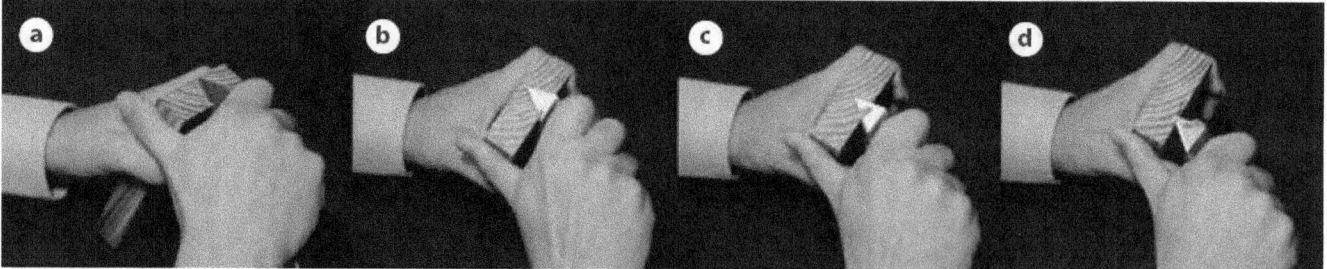

Figure 4.7—Safely making the cut. (a) The grip of the specimen and knife and the placement of fingers and thumbs. (b–d) The progress of the knife through the specimen. The cut begins at the base of the knife (a, b) and the knife is pulled through the specimen, drawing the edge along the wood as the cut is made. Note that at the end of the cut, the tip of the blade is all that is in contact with the wood (d). In all images, the thumb of the knife hand is below the top surface of the specimen (shown clearly in a).

utility knife begins to feel dull, replace it. As your technique improves, blades will last longer, but in the beginning you will use several blades in a few hours of cutting and observing wood.

At first you may lack the physical strength needed to make clean cuts of wood, but this will come with practice as you exercise those muscles. Physical strength is far less important than good technique, but your strength will increase with practice. If either of your hands are feeling weak or beginning to fatigue, stop practicing and allow your strength to return before you continue; shaking your hands to loosen them can be helpful. Controlling the progress of the blade through the wood depends on technique, but fatigue can cause sloppy technique and result in injury, so you must not cut if your hands are tired.

▶ You are almost ready to try to cut a specimen; read the section on inspecting the cut first.

4.7 Inspecting the cut
Now you have made a cut. Specifically, you have exposed one of the planes of section of the wood, the transverse surface. Inspect it with your hand lens (Fig. 4.8). Pay special attention to the plane you produced and its orientation with respect to the cells; the cells of the axial system should be nearly perpendicular to your cut. If they are not, you must

make a new cut, taking special care to orient the edge of the blade at the angle that will produce a true transverse plane. For a tangential plane of section, your cut surface must be perpendicular to the rays as seen on the transverse surface. It must follow the cells of the axial system and it must cut along rather than across the grain.

▶ Now you may cut a transverse surface on your practice specimen.

4.8 Cutting with a razor blade
For soft or low-density woods, a utility knife is the wrong tool for the job, and you will need to use a razor blade. The basic principles of cutting and the safety rules are the same for this tool as for a utility knife. You will hold the specimen the same way as well. The only differences are in how to hold the razor blade, and the direction of the cutting motion. Razor blades are not strong implements, and when using them you do not need the force used with a utility knife. Simply pinch the razor blade firmly between your thumb and forefinger, and push (not pull) the blade from the corner of the specimen across the wood to produce a clean surface. Focus on safety, and allow the blade (rather than brute force) to cut the specimen.

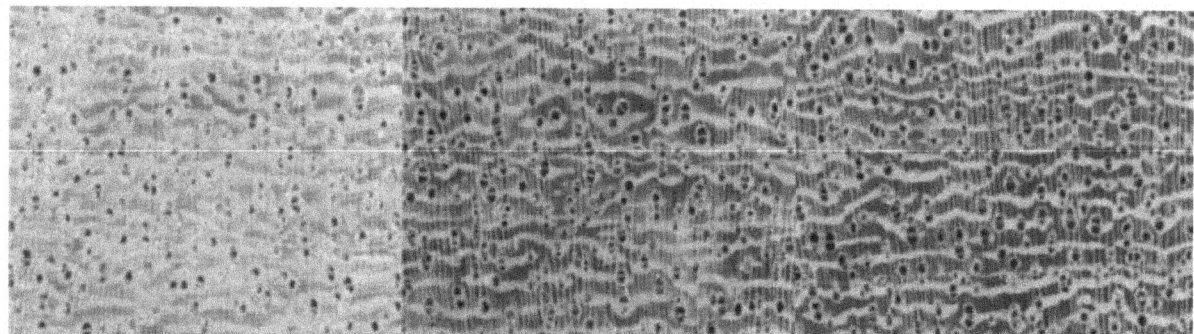

Figure 4.8—Cuts of different quality. The left image shows the specimen cut with a sharp table saw. The middle image shows the specimen cut cleanly with a utility knife. The right image shows the specimen prepared in a laboratory, resulting in a research-quality image.

5 | Basic characters used in the identification of wood with a hand lens

The characters presented in this chapter represent the minimal set of terms and concepts necessary to build skill and proficiency in wood identification with a hand lens. This list is not exhaustive, nor is it in complete agreement with the characters used by other authors, in other references, or in traditional microscopic wood anatomy. The ways in which these characters and definitions deviate from other authors are not important for our purposes, but it is important to note that if you also use other wood identification references, you must compare those authors' definitions of characters to those you learn here. The approach of this manual was chosen based on experience teaching hand lens wood identification at various workshops in Central America, Asia, and the United States. The intent here is to streamline the learning process and have you working with real wood specimens as quickly as possible. As you use this manual in the field, you will doubtless come across characters from species not covered here. Make note of what you see and compare it to the characters outlined below. If, after careful study and observation, you are certain you have found something not described here, that is excellent; it means you have learned not only the meaning of the characters here, but also have gained wisdom sufficient to understand that you are seeing something new.

5.1 Anatomical characters in wood identification

The identification portions of this manual focus on the use of anatomical characteristics to identify unknown wood specimens. With the basic biology of wood familiar to you from the section on wood biology, we will now revisit the cells and structures and define them as characters for identification. In each case, we will be thinking of the structures as either being present or absent in a specimen. This process requires constant observation and questioning: is the character present or absent, or is it impossible to tell? The

difference between understanding wood anatomy as a biological field and interpreting that anatomy as characters for identification is a subtle but important one.

The images throughout the manual are not perfect; they show marks left by the knives that cut them or the sander that smoothed them for photography. Rather than try to explain away the difference between perfect images and surfaces you can produce in the real world, more realistic photos of wood are shown in this manual, especially in Chapter 7. In many of the images presented, the notation "M" describes the artifacts of preparation in addition to the anatomical features. As you become proficient in the preparation and observation of wood specimens, you will train your mind to ignore artifacts like knife marks, but in the initial phases of learning these skills, knife marks can appear to the untrained eye as actual anatomical structures.

5.1.1 Softwood or hardwood?
The first question to ask yourself when confronting an unknown wood specimen is whether it is a softwood or a hardwood. Softwoods are defined anatomically by the absence of vessels (pores), and hardwoods by their presence (Fig. 5.1).

5.1.2 Softwoods
For the softwoods treated in this manual, only two anatomical features can be observed with a hand lens—the presence or absence of resin canals and the characteristics of the transition within the growth rings. Both of these features are seen on the transverse surface.

Resin canals
Resin canals are the structures that produce pitch or resin and are found in *Pinus, Picea, Larix,* and *Pseudotsuga.* When you are first learning wood identification, resin canals can look much like vessels in hardwoods, but there are two easy

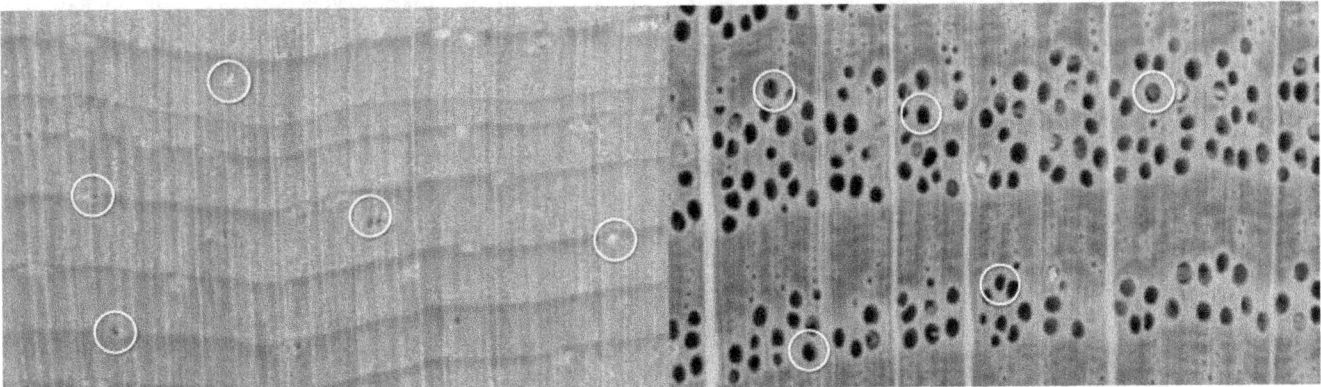

Figure 5.1—Distinguishing softwoods from hardwoods based on the absence or presence of vessels. In the softwood on the left, there are no vessels, but several resin canals are circled. In the hardwood on the right, several vessels are circled. Note that the general appearance, number, and distribution of vessels and resin canals are quite different. With practice, you will automatically recognize the characteristics that distinguish vessels from resin canals.

ways to differentiate them. First, resin canals, if present at all, are usually found in the latewood or in the area between the earlywood and the latewood. Vessels in hardwoods will be found in all portions of the growth ring. Second, even in softwoods with many resin canals, there are still far fewer resin canals in a hand lens view than there are vessels in most hardwoods. With some practice, especially comparing a hardwood and a softwood with resin canals side by side, these specific differences will not be important; you will recognize the pattern of a softwood with or without resin canals and you will not confuse resin canals with vessels.

Growth ring transitions

In the growth rings of softwoods, the transition from earlywood to latewood can be abrupt, gradual, or absent (Fig. 5.2a–c). In woods with abrupt transition, there is a clearly visible zone where the tracheid cell wall thickness changes from thin-walled earlywood cells to thick-walled latewood cells (Fig. 5.2a). A gradual transition from earlywood to latewood is one in which the tracheid cell wall thickness becomes slightly greater toward the latewood but with no clear line where the earlywood ends and the latewood begins (Fig. 5.2b). No transition between earlywood and latewood is comparatively rare in softwoods and is generally only seen in tropical species that lack obvious growth rings (Fig. 5.2c).

5.1.3 Hardwoods

As mentioned earlier, the anatomical variability of hardwoods is many times greater than that of softwoods, and much of this variability can be seen with a hand lens.

Growth rings

There are three classifications of growth rings in hardwoods, depending on transitions in the relative size, pattern, distribution, or abundance of vessels. The three classifications are ring-porous, semi-ring-porous, and diffuse porous (Fig. 5.2d–f).

In ring-porous woods, the earlywood vessels are distinctly larger (usually from 3 to 10 times the diameter) than the latewood vessels, and also commonly more closely packed together (Fig. 5.2d). The transition between large earlywood vessels and much smaller latewood vessels is distinct.

Semi-ring-porous woods are like ring-porous woods in that the earlywood vessels are large and the latewood vessels are half the diameter or smaller, but unlike ring-porous woods, there is a gradual rather than distinct decrease in vessel diameter from the earlywood through the latewood. This results in a clear distinction between the latewood of one growth ring and the earlywood of the next, but in no clear distinction between the earlywood and latewood within the same growth ring (Fig. 5.2e). Semi-ring-porous woods are used comparatively rarely in timber bridges.

Diffuse-porous woods, the most common type of hardwood, do not show a large difference in diameter between earlywood and latewood vessels. From the beginning of a growth ring to the end, the vessels are more or less evenly distributed and are of similar size, though in many diffuse-porous woods there will be a slight decrease in vessel diameter in the latewood (Fig. 5.2f). This small difference in diameter should not be confused with the semi-ring-porous pattern, in which the difference is substantial.

Vessel arrangement

Vessel arrangement is a term used to describe the pattern, if any, of vessels within a growth ring. This is different from the concept of growth ring classification. Most woods have a random or even distribution of vessels in the wood; this pattern is not generally considered worthy of a special name as a character, because it is the assumed default condition. The concept of vessel arrangement involves two distinct aspects: the number of vessels in contact with each other and the distribution of vessels throughout the growth ring.

When vessels occur one at a time and are not in contact with other vessels, they are called solitary vessels (Fig. 5.3a). Most woods have at least a few solitary vessels, but comparatively few woods have exclusively solitary vessels; when this character is present, it is a strong character. When two or more vessels are touching each other and extend in the radial direction (parallel to the rays), they form a vessel multiple. Vessel multiples are commonly formed from two to four vessels (Fig. 5.3b); multiples with more than four vessels are less common. When several vessels are in contact radially and tangentially, they form vessel clusters. Vessel clusters are much less common than vessel multiples, and thus the presence of this character is a useful one for identification.

Vessels, whether solitary, in multiples, or in clusters, can also have patterns of distribution within the growth ring that receive special names. One pattern is radially aligned vessels and occurs when vessels are organized into radial lines or files, often lined up between rays. This pattern can occur in woods with solitary, multiple, or clustered vessels, though it is most common in the former two than the latter. A related pattern is vessels arranged in echelon (Fig. 5.3c); this is like radial arrangement, but instead of running parallel to the rays, the vessels form a pattern at a diagonal to the rays. The last pattern is called dendritic vessel arrangement (Fig. 5.3d), and is characterized by v-shaped, flame-shaped, or tree-like groups of vessels that are narrower on the pith side of the growth ring (toward the earlywood) and widen out toward the bark side (toward and into the latewood). It is important to note that several different vessel arrangements can be present in one wood at the same time.

Rays

As mentioned earlier, rays in hardwoods can be narrow like those of softwoods, or quite wide (Fig. 5.4). They can also be numerous, or a species can have few rays. These characters are best observed from the transverse surface, can be critical in hardwood identification, and are a major part of the wood anatomical pattern. Because the concepts of narrow, wide,

Softwoods   Hardwoods

Growth ring transitions

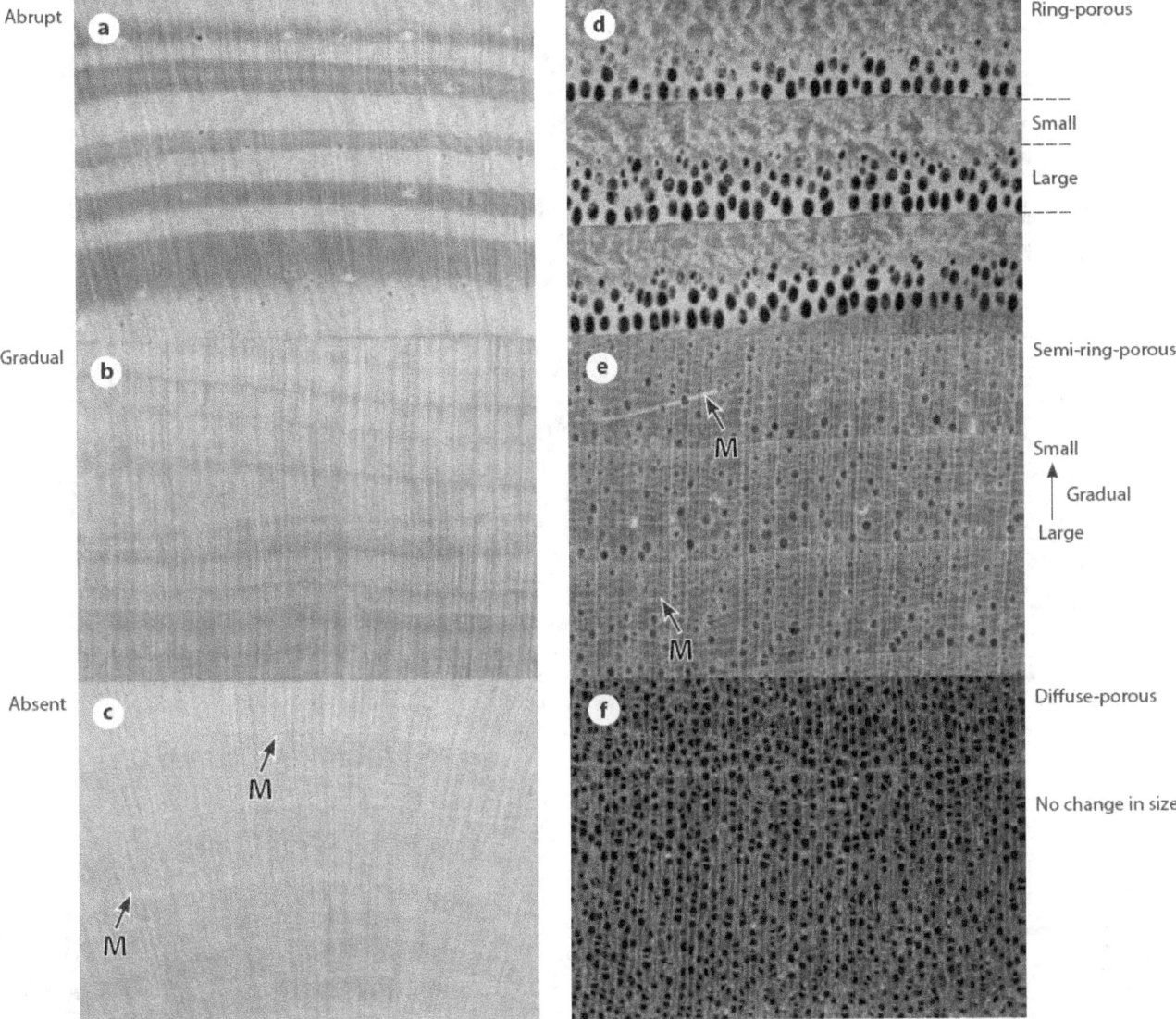

Figure 5.2—Growth ring classifications in softwoods (a–c) and hardwoods (d–f). (a) Abrupt transition within a growth ring from the earlywood to latewood is the most common transition type in the softwoods in this manual. Note how the earlywood appears lighter in color than the latewood, and how the change from earlywood to latewood happens at a distinct place in the growth ring. (b) Gradual transition from earlywood to latewood results in a subtler pattern. (c) No transition within a growth ring is not seen in any of the softwoods in this manual. (d) Ring-porous hardwoods show an abrupt change in vessel diameter at the boundary between the earlywood and the latewood. (e) Semi-ring-porous hardwoods show a gradual reduction of vessel diameter from earlywood to latewood. (f) Diffuse-porous hardwoods, the most common type of growth ring transition in the woods in this manual, show no clear change in vessel size or distribution from the earlywood to the latewood, and sometimes lack obvious growth rings altogether.

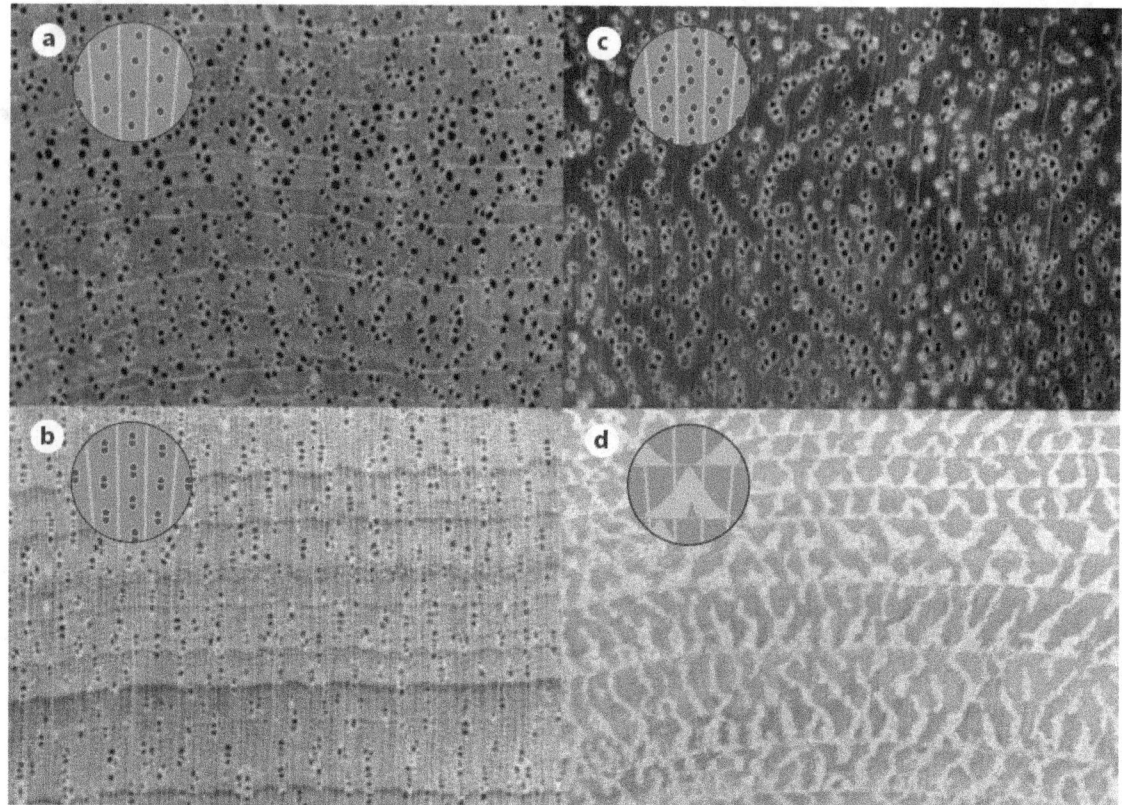

Figure 5.3—Patterns in vessel arrangement. (a) Solitary vessels are those that are not in contact with other vessels. They usually appear distinctly rounded. (b) Vessel multiples are groups of two or more vessels with cell walls in contact. The individual vessels in a vessel multiple often appear slightly flattened where the two vessels touch. (c) Vessels in echelon arrangement can be either solitary vessels, vessel multiples, or a combination of both. The pattern of echelon vessel arrangement must be observed over a wider area, because it is a pattern formed by many vessels and how they are arranged relative to the direction of the rays. (d) Dendritic vessel arrangement is rare or absent in the woods in this manual, and it usually found in woods with extremely small-diameter vessels. Most of the vessels in this image are too small to see individually with a hand lens.

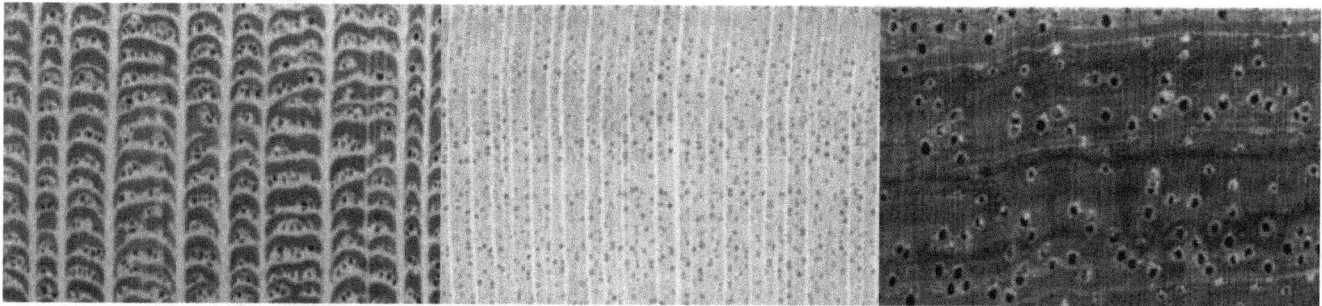

Figure 5.4—Differences in ray width and ray number. The image on the left shows comparatively few, wide rays; however, careful observation will show that there are narrow rays between the wide rays. Observing only the wide rays, this wood has few rays. The middle image shows a wood with an average number and size of rays. The image on the right shows a wood with numerous, narrow rays.

few, and numerous are easily understood by examining photos or transverse surfaces of a variety of hardwoods, little explanation is needed.

Axial parenchyma patterns

Axial parenchyma patterns in hardwoods are critical characters used in wood identification. Axial parenchyma patterns can be divided into three broad groups, depending on the position and appearance of the parenchyma (Fig. 5.5).

The first type of axial parenchyma is called marginal parenchyma. This name is used because marginal parenchyma occurs at the beginning or end of a growth ring, and when present assists in defining the growth rings of the wood. Marginal parenchyma appears as a solid line of cells running evenly around the growth ring (Fig. 5.5 top); it generally does not have a wavy or undulating appearance. With some practice, correctly determining the presence of marginal parenchyma is an easy task.

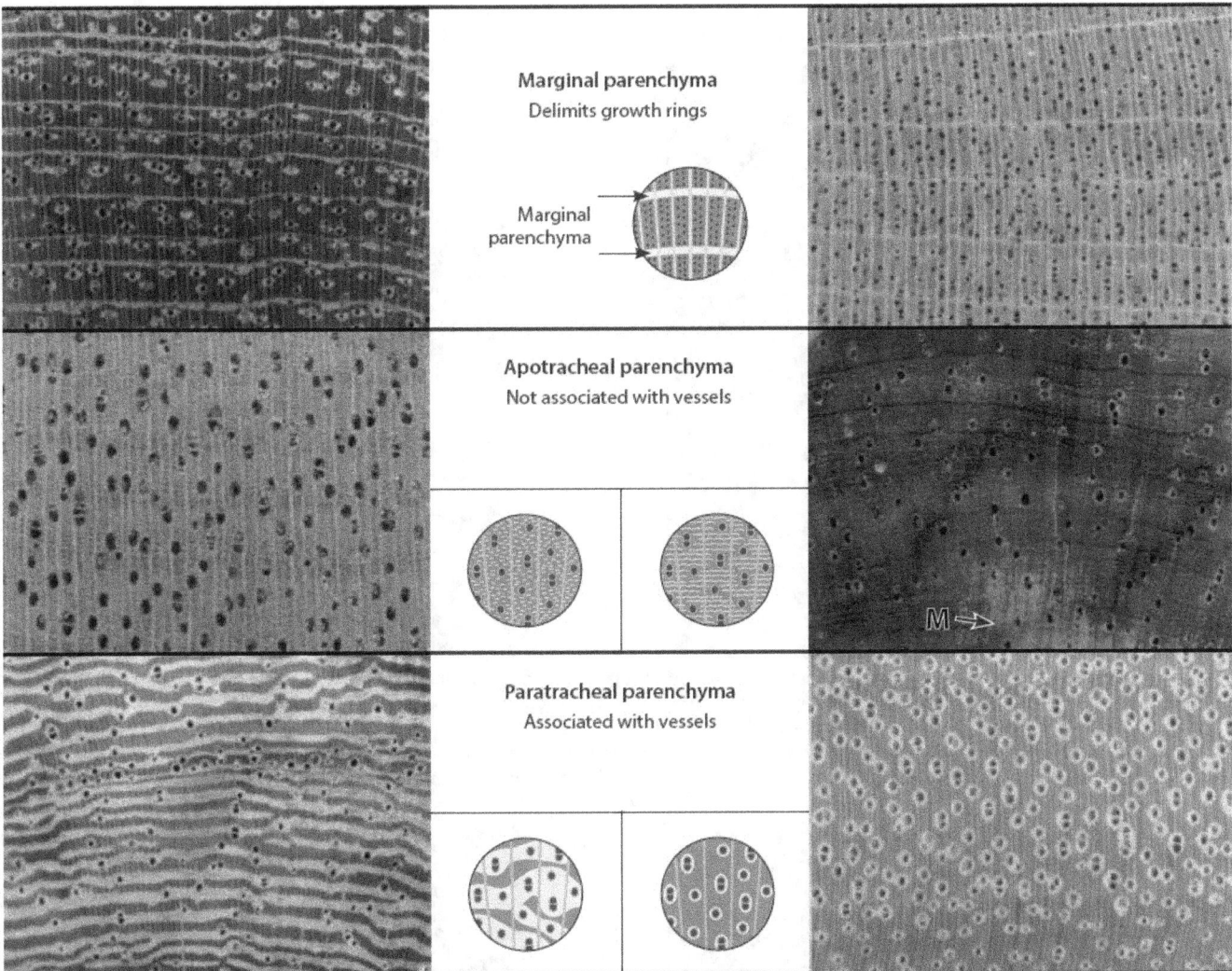

Figure 5.5—There are three types of axial parenchyma in hardwoods: marginal, apotracheal, and paratracheal. Marginal parenchyma occurs at the beginning or end of a growth ring, and is shown in the top images and illustrations. Both apotracheal and paratracheal parenchyma occur within the growth ring, and differ on the basis of their association with vessels. Apotracheal parenchyma is not associated with vessels, and is shown in the middle images and illustrations. Paratracheal parenchyma is closely associated with vessels, and is shown in the bottom images and illustrations.

Whereas marginal parenchyma is defined as delimiting the boundary of a growth ring, the other two types of parenchyma are defined on the basis of their association or lack of association with vessels and occur within the body of the growth ring. If the parenchyma is not associated with the vessels, it is called apotracheal parenchyma (Fig. 5.5 middle). If it is associated with vessels, it is called paratracheal (Fig. 5.5 bottom). The idea of association with vessels is at first a somewhat complex one, as will be seen below. Learning the names and patterns of apotracheal and paratracheal parenchyma, and having the words mean the correct things in your mind, is one of the hardest aspects of learning the characters for wood identification.

Apotracheal parenchyma is parenchyma not associated with the vessels, and occurs in three basic patterns: diffuse, diffuse-in-aggregate, and banded. These three patterns can be considered part of a continuum (Fig. 5.6b–d); at one end is diffuse apotracheal parenchyma, in the middle is diffuse-in-aggregate apotracheal parenchyma, and at the other end is banded apotracheal parenchyma. Diffuse apotracheal parenchyma appears as small dots of generally lighter colored cells scattered out in the fibers and not touching the vessels (Fig. 5.6b). Diffuse apotracheal parenchyma is often not visible with a hand lens and so will only be used as a character in species that show it clearly. Diffuse-in-aggregate apotracheal parenchyma has a similar distribution, but instead of single cells, is formed of small tangential lines of two to four cells (Fig. 5.6c). This gives it the appearance of short, broken lines of cells running perpendicular to the rays, but still not associated with vessels. The aggregates of cells do not usually cross the rays, contributing to its broken appearance. In contrast to diffuse-in-aggregate apotracheal parenchyma, banded apotracheal parenchyma is formed of long, wavy lines of cells typically crossing several to many rays (Fig. 5.6d). Depending on the length of the bands, they may appear to be touching

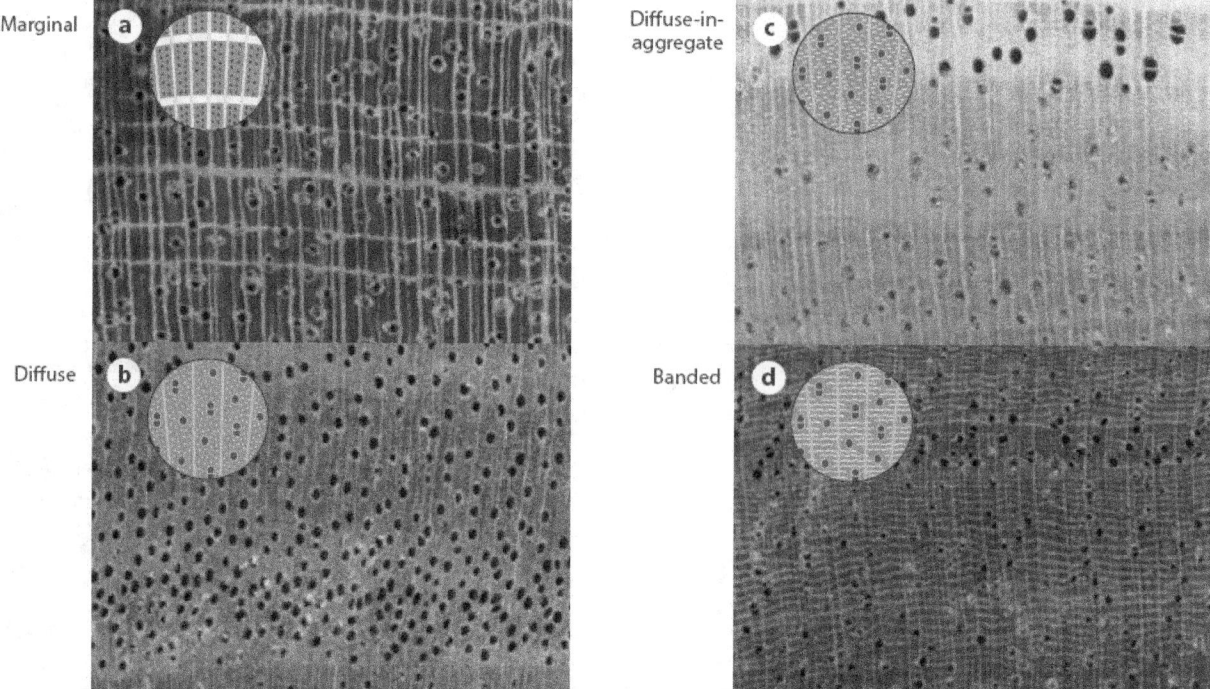

Figure 5.6—Specific axial parenchyma patterns. (a) Marginal parenchyma. Note that the bands of marginal parenchyma are thick. (b) Diffuse apotracheal parenchyma; this, when observable with a hand lens, appears as small dots among the fibers. (c) Diffuse-in-aggregate apotracheal parenchyma appears as short tangential lines among the fibers, and the short lines generally do not cross the rays. (d) Banded apotracheal parenchyma forms long tangential lines among the fibers, the bands typically cross several rays, and are often wavy. Compare this pattern to marginal parenchyma in (a).

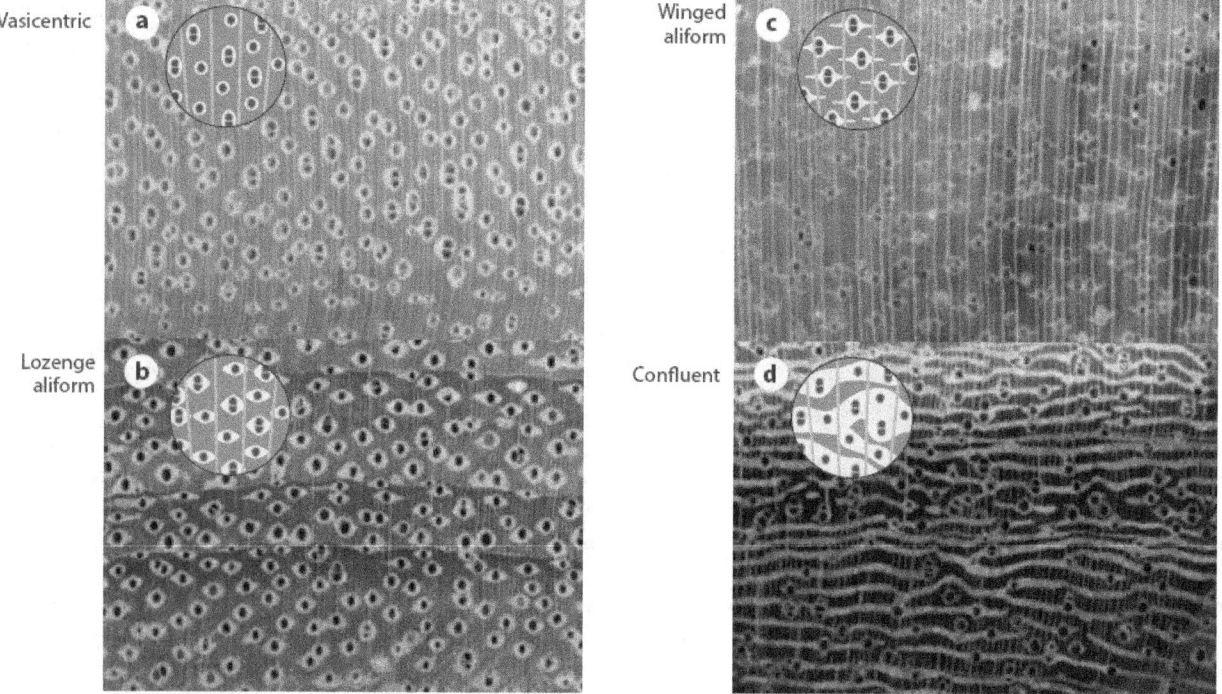

Figure 5.7—Specific axial parenchyma patterns. (a) Vasicentric paratracheal parenchyma appears as an even sheath or halo of parenchyma around the vessels or vessel multiples. (b) Lozenge aliform paratracheal parenchyma appears similar to vasicentric parenchyma, but the parenchyma surrounding the vessels extends tangentially with short, thick projections. (c) Winged aliform paratracheal parenchyma is most similar to lozenge aliform parenchyma, but with narrow, long wings extending tangentially. (d) Confluent paratracheal parenchyma appears like a series of vessels connected by lozenge aliform or winged aliform parenchyma. The connecting, tangential bands of parenchyma can be narrow or wide, and can connect from two to several hundred vessels. Compare this to banded apotracheal parenchyma in Figure 5.6d and note the differences in association of parenchyma with the vessels.

vessels. You can think of this pattern, when it contacts vessels, as being interrupted by them, rather than associated with them. Individual bands can be from many millimeters in length tangentially to less than half a millimeter in length. Bands can also be narrow (a single cell) radially, or wide (many cells).

Paratracheal parenchyma is always clearly associated with the vessels, has a variety of patterns, and much like apotracheal parenchyma, these patterns can be seen as a part of a continuum (Fig. 5.7). At one end of the spectrum is vasicentric paratracheal parenchyma, in the middle is aliform paratracheal parenchyma, and at the other end is confluent paratracheal parenchyma. Vasicentric paratracheal parenchyma appears as a round halo or sheath of parenchyma around the vessel, and it can be narrow or wide, referring to distance out from the vessel it extends (Fig. 5.7a). Aliform paratracheal parenchyma is like vasicentric paratracheal parenchyma with tangential extensions. That is, there are extensions from the sheath of parenchyma perpendicular to the rays. These extensions can be comparatively long and narrow, giving a winged aliform paratracheal parenchyma pattern (Fig. 5.7c), or thicker and short, giving a lozenge aliform paratracheal parenchyma pattern (Fig. 5.7b). If the wings of aliform paratracheal parenchyma stretch outward and fuse with the wings of adjacent aliform paratracheal parenchyma from another vessel, the pattern formed is called confluent paratracheal parenchyma (Fig. 5.7d). Confluent paratracheal parenchyma can connect as few as two

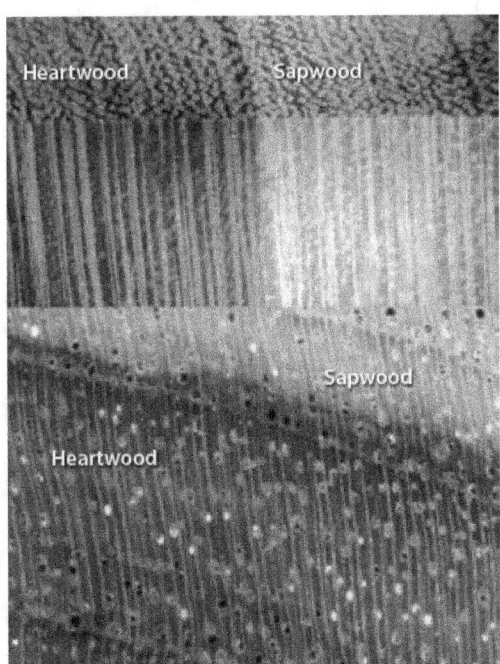

Figure 5.8—Heartwood color is derived from chemicals deposited by the tree as it matures. The top image shows the heartwood–sapwood transition; the sapwood is yellower in color, and the heartwood reddish. The bottom image shows a heartwood–sapwood transition in another wood; the sapwood is whitish, and heartwood a rich brown.

vessels or hundreds of vessels. The radial thickness of the parenchyma between vessels can be narrow or wide.

5.1.4 Vessel contents
Although wood identification has many additional anatomical terms and characters, only three more are necessary to complete our working list of characters used in this manual, and all pertain to materials that can be found in vessels: tyloses, gums, and powders. For all three, they are typically found only in heartwood; if you are examining sapwood of a species for any of the three, you will not find them. Tyloses are outgrowths of parenchyma cells into vessels and appear in the vessels as bubbles or shiny, angled inclusions. Gums are resinous, shiny, sticky-looking, generally dark materials that appear to plug the vessels. Powders are like gums, but appear as dry, dusty, or powdery materials, and are generally lighter in color.

5.2 Nonanatomical characters in wood identification
The characters used in wood identification are primarily anatomical ones, though there are some nonanatomical features that will be referenced in the identification key (Chapter 6). These nonanatomical characters include color, odor, density and hardness, regularity of grain, and fluorescence.

5.2.1 Color
Color in wood usually refers to the heartwood color (Fig. 5.8) and is a difficult topic to discuss for several reasons. The heartwood color in a freshly felled log may be quite different from the color of the heartwood once the wood has been dried and processed. Many woods change color over time and with exposure to light (e.g., American black cherry, *Prunus serotina*) even after they are dried and processed. There can also be significant natural biological variability (a wide range of colors) in the color of a given species or timber. Some species have characteristic streaks of color throughout the heartwood that are not always present in small specimens. A further complication is that people see colors differently, and words to describe color often do not mean exactly the same thing to different people. For these reasons, the information presented about the color of woods should be interpreted loosely. Additionally, the color of a timber in a bridge, at least partly exposed to dirt, dust, light, and the elements, may bear no semblance at all to the "natural" color of the same wood.

5.2.2 Odor
Odor in wood is another nonanatomical character that can be both valuable and difficult to describe. As with color, different people will perceive the odor of the same wood differently, and there can be significant variability in the strength of the odor of wood. Generally speaking, odor is not a strong character, and should only be used at the end of an identification, when all anatomical characters have been observed. As with color, the exposure of timbers in a bridge

may result in a characteristic odor being absent or masked by other scents, such as mold, decay, or chemical treatment (e.g., the odor of creosote will overpower any natural scent in wood).

5.2.3 Density and hardness

Density and hardness are related physical properties of wood and have strong influences on the mechanical properties, and thus on the ultimate strength attributed to the members in a bridge. Density describes the weight or mass of a specimen compared to its volume, and hardness gives information about how easy or difficult it is to cut or dent the wood. The apparent density of a piece of wood is affected by the amount of moisture in the specimen; wood left out in the rain will soak up water and seem denser than wood of the same species that has been properly dried. For this reason, density is best used as a character only when it is clearly quite high or quite low. Most woods are of a medium or average density, and in such species density is not a useful character. The same thing is true of hardness; if the wood is easy to dent with your fingernail, it is soft. If you cannot dent it with your fingernail, it is hard. Remember that hardness or softness are physical properties of the wood, and have nothing to do with whether the wood is a softwood or a hardwood, terms that refer to the botanical origin of the wood and the kinds of cells you will see in them. For both density and hardness, evaluation of these properties is only meaningful for sound wood. Wood that is decayed or otherwise damaged may seem lighter or softer than the species would normally be.

5.2.4 Regularity of grain

Regularity of grain refers to whether the cells of the axial system of the wood are wavy, interlocked, or straight. Wavy grain occurs when the cells of the axial system run up and down the trunk of the tree with gradual back-and-forth undulations of maybe 1–2 cm. Interlocked grain is formed when the cells of the axial system do not run perfectly straight up and down the tree but rather grow curving up the tree to the right for several years, then curve up the tree to the left for several years, then back to the right. This alternating pattern of curvature up the trunk produces wood that can be quite attractive (especially in species with luster, like *Ulmus* (elm), where interlocked grain is common), but is also difficult to process, and sometimes problematic to prepare for hand lens observation because the angle of the grain in one part of specimen is often quite different from the angle in a different part. Straight-grained wood is neither wavy nor interlocked; the cells of the axial system are straight and run up and down the trunk nearly vertically. The regularity of grain is generally not a strong character in wood identification, but can affect strength properties of timbers.

5.2.5 Fluorescence

A last nonanatomical character is fluorescence. If you shine a UV lamp (either a small portable light or a larger laboratory model) on freshly sanded or cut surfaces, some woods fluoresce. That is, the slightly purple or invisible UV light is taken up by the specimen and a different color (usually a yellow-green color) is emitted by the wood. This is most easily seen in dark conditions. Most woods lack fluorescence, so it can be a powerful character for confirming an identification once an initial determination is made based on wood anatomical features, but it can be difficult to assess in the field. Exposure to the elements can render a normally fluorescent wood no longer fluorescent, and some decay fungi produce yellow-fluorescent compounds in nonfluorescent woods.

With practice and experience, all the nonanatomical features discussed above will play a part in your identification of a wood specimen. Because nonanatomical features are generally much weaker than anatomical ones, you will tend to use them either as secondary confirmations or as an automatic part of pattern recognition, where you do not specifically ask yourself "Does this specimen have a pinkish cast to its heartwood?" but rather notice automatically whether or not it has this characteristic. That is to say, nonanatomical characters are often some of the first characters that will form a part of the artistic aspect of wood identification.

6 | Identification key

6.1 How to use the key

The key is written to guide you through the identification process in the most efficient and accurate way possible. It presents you with a numbered series of questions. The answers you provide will be based on your interpretations of the anatomical characters in your unknown specimen and will lead you to a new set of questions. Each time you answer a question and proceed to the next you are one step closer to making an identification. Eventually, the key will direct you to a species depicted in Chapter 7. If your specimen is a good match for the indicated wood, you have successfully identified it. If, however, your unknown specimen is a species not included in the key, the images and information in Chapter 7 will not match, and you must conclude that the specimen is not recognized. This will happen from time to time, because no key includes all woods. In such an event, seek the assistance of trained wood identification expert.

6.2 Key to common woods in covered timber bridges

Number	Key features to evaluate	Go to	Common name	Scientific name
1	Vessels absent (softwood)	2		
1	Vessels present (hardwood)	11		
2	Resin canals present	3		
2	Resin canals absent	9		
3	Growth ring transition abrupt	4		
3	Growth ring transition gradual	8		
4	Resin canals large/conspicuous	5		
4	Resin canals small/inconspicuous	7		
5	Earlywood often more than half the width of the growth ring	6		
5	Earlywood typically less than half the growth ring, heartwood yellowish to brown, southern origin		Southern Yellow Pine Group	*Pinus* sp., Southern yellow pine group (p. 30)
6	Heartwood with a pinkish cast, northern origin		Red Pine	*Pinus resinosa* (p. 31)
6	Heartwood brownish or yellowish, western or northern origin		Yellow Pine Group (not Southern)	*Pinus* sp., yellow pine group (p. 32)
7	Resin canals occurring singly, heartwood generally yellowish in color		Larch/Tamarack	*Larix* sp. (p. 33)
7	Resin canals occurring singly and in pairs, heartwood generally with a faint pinkish cast		Douglas-fir	*Pseudotsuga* cf. *mensiezii* (p. 34)
8	Resin canals large/conspicuous		Soft Pine Group; if Eastern origin, Eastern White Pine	*Pinus* sp., soft pine group; *Pinus strobus* if Eastern origin (p. 35)
8	Resin canals small/inconspicuous		Spruce	*Picea* sp. (p. 36)
9	Growth ring transition abrupt	10		
9	Growth ring transition gradual		If an Eastern wood, use NDS "Eastern Softwoods." If a Western wood, use NDS "Western Woods."	

6.2 Key to common woods in covered timber bridges—con.

Number	Key features to evaluate	Go to	Common name	Scientific name
10	Southeastern wood, heartwood yellowish to brown, often oily		Baldcypress	*Taxodium distichum* (p. 37)
10	Western wood, heartwood distinctly reddish in color, without cedar odor		Redwood	*Sequoiadendron/ Sequoia* sp. (p. 38)
11	Wood ring-porous or semi-ring-porous	12		
11	Wood diffuse-porous	19		
12	Rays narrow and with frequent broad rays (1 mm wide or wider) interspersed, the broad rays easily seen with the naked eye	13		
12	Rays narrow to medium width	14		
13	Latewood vessels comparatively large, solitary, rounded in outline		Red Oak Group	*Quercus* sp., red oak group (p. 39)
13	Latewood vessels small, in clusters or flame-like arrangement (dendritic), not clearly rounded in outline		White Oak Group	*Quercus* sp., white oak group (p. 40)
14	Latewood mostly composed of prominent, long, wavy, tangential bands of tiny vessels		Elm or Hackberry	*Ulmus* sp. or *Celtis* sp. (p. 41)
14	Latewood not mostly composed of vessels in wavy tangential bands	15		
15	Latewood parenchyma pattern predominantly apotracheal banded	16		
15	Latewood parenchyma pattern not predominantly apotracheal banded	17		
16	Wood ring-porous, hard and heavy		Hickory/Pecan	*Carya* sp. (p. 42)
16	Wood semi-ring-porous, medium density		Walnut/Butternut	*Juglans* sp. (p. 43)
17	Rays narrow and numerous, not usually visible without a lens	18		
17	Rays of medium width, often distinct without a lens—everything else northern woods	19		
18	Latewood vessels with faint sheath of aliform paratracheal parenchyma, latest latewood vessels very small, embedded in confluent parenchyma, polychromatic tyloses in earlywood vessels common, wood hard and moderately heavy		Ash	*Fraxinus* sp. (p. 44)
18	Latewood vessels with faint sheath of aliform paratracheal parenchyma, latest latewood vessels very small, embedded in confluent parenchyma, polychromatic tyloses in earlywood vessels common, wood is soft and light, with a greyish cast		Catalpa	*Catalpa* sp. (p. 45)
18	Latewood vessels in flame-shaped (dendritic) groups, earlywood vessel commonly with tyloses		Chestnut	*Castanea* sp. (p. 46)

6.2 Key to common woods in covered timber bridges—con.

Number	Key features to evaluate	Go to	Common name	Scientific name
19	Rays all or frequently wide, some woods with occasional broad rays of the oak type between narrower rays	20		
19	Rays narrow or up to medium width, numerous or few	21		
20	All rays medium to wide, wood soft to medium-hard		Sycamore	*Platanus occidentalis* (p. 47)
20	Most rays narrow to medium width, occasional broad rays of the oak type, such broad rays commonly flared or fluted at growth ring boundaries		Beech	*Fagus grandifolia* (p. 48)
20	Rare presence of a wide, disorganized ray, otherwise rays barely visible		Alder	*Alnus* sp. (p. 49)
21	Vessels extremely numerous, quite small and often difficult to distinguish with a hand lens		Unrecognized hardwood	No scientific name (p. 50)
21	Vessels abundant but easy to distinguish with hand lens	22		
22	Wood moderately hard and heavy, with marginal parenchyma	23		
22	Wood comparatively soft and lower density	24		
23	Wood whitish to light brown		Maple or Birch	*Acer* sp. or *Betula* sp. (p. 51)
23	Wood light to dark green to black, often with luster		Yellow Poplar or Magnolia	*Liriodendron tulipifera* or *Magnolia* sp. (p. 52)
24	Wood whitish to light brown	25		
24	Wood light to dark green to black, often with luster		Yellow Poplar or Magnolia	*Liriodendron tulipifera* or *Magnolia* sp. (p. 52)
25	Wood with marginal and banded apotracheal or diffuse-in-aggregate parenchymya		Basswood	*Tilia* sp. (p. 53)
25	Wood with only marginal parenchyma		Aspen/Poplar/Cottonwood	*Populus* sp. (p. 54)

6.3 Checklist of features

A checklist like the one below can be helpful when identifying an unknown specimen, because it encourages you to go through the process of observing specific features useful in wood identification. It can prevent you from overlooking an important character or failing to check for the presence of all possible features. With practice and experience, such a checklist will be less useful to you for wood patterns you recognize automatically, but it can help with difficult specimens even when you have years of practice identifying wood.

Softwoods (vessels absent)			Present or absent?
Resin canals			
Growth ring transition	Abrupt		
	Gradual		
Hardwoods (vessels present)			**Present or absent?**
Growth rings	Ring-porous		
	Semi-ring-porous		
	Diffuse-porous		
Vessel arrangement	Solitary		
	Multiples		
	Clusters		
	Radial		
	Echelon		
	Wavy tangential bands (ulmiform latewood)		
Vessel contents	Powders (white, yellow, etc.)		
	Tyloses		
	Gums or resins		
Vessel size	Small		
	Medium		
	Large		
Rays	Numerous		
	Few		
	Wide		
	Narrow		
Axial parenchyma	Marginal		
	Apotracheal	Diffuse	
		Diffuse-in-aggregate	
		Banded	
	Paratracheal	Vasicentric	
		Aliform	
		Confluent	
Growth rings per cm	Many		
	Few		

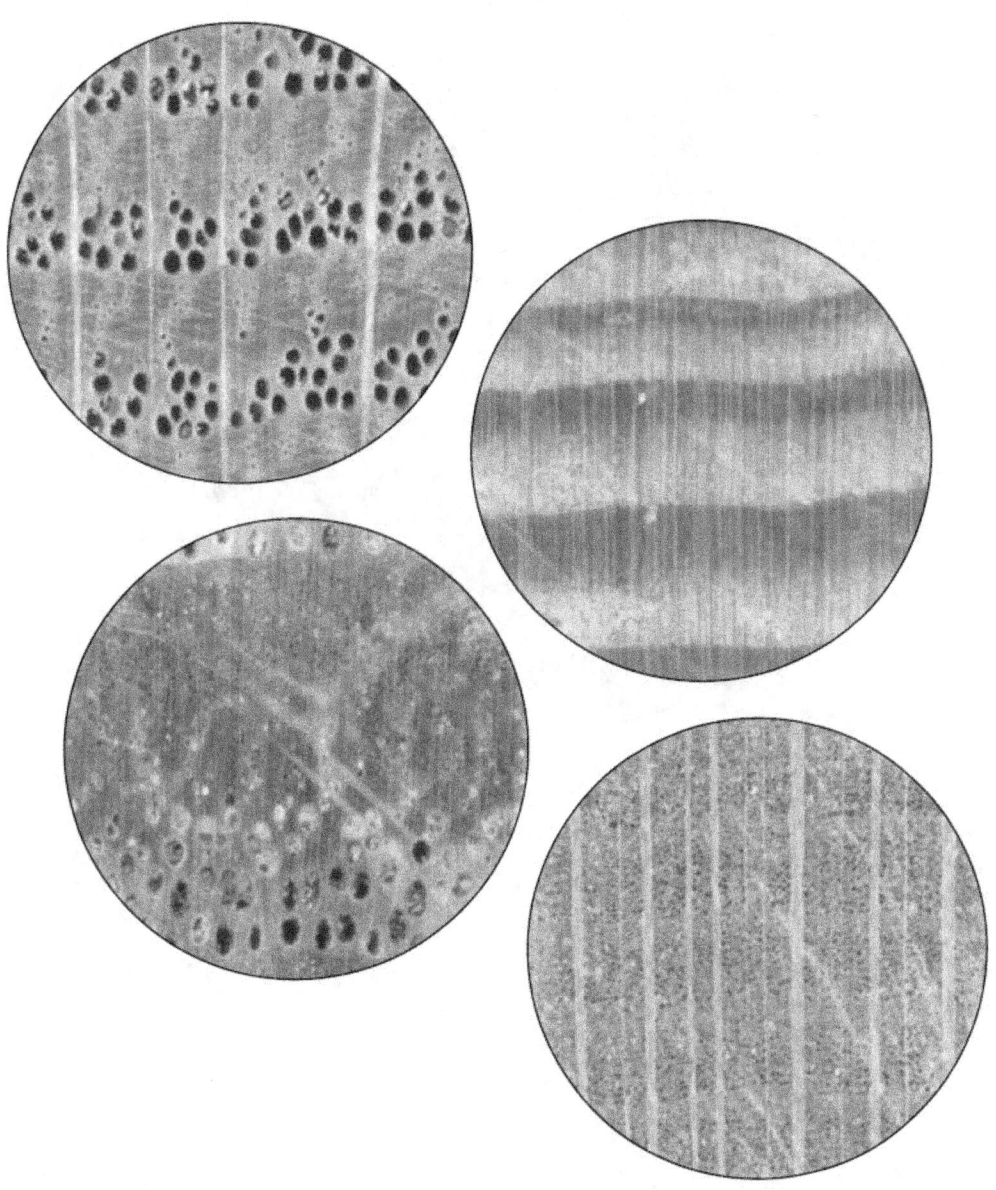

Southern Yellow Pine Group

Pinus sp., Southern yellow pine group

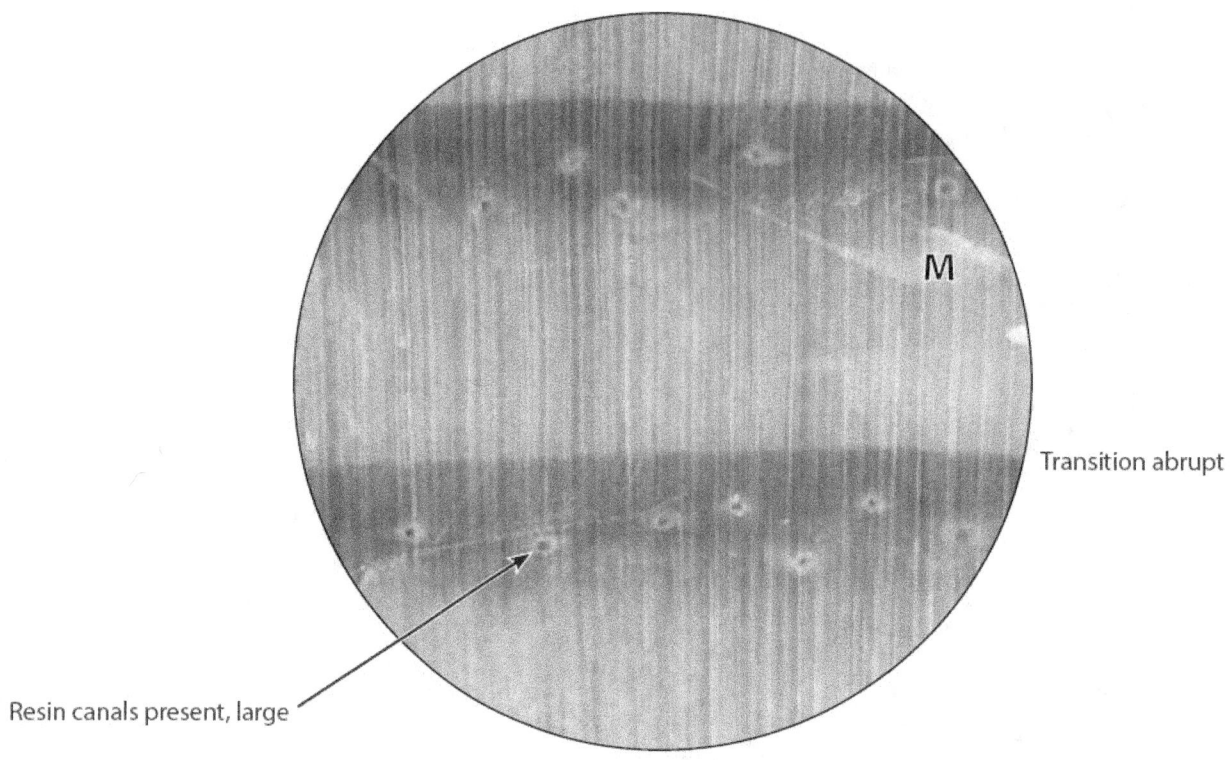

M

Transition abrupt

Resin canals present, large

National Design Specification guidance

Use the Southern Pine NDS designation.

Notes

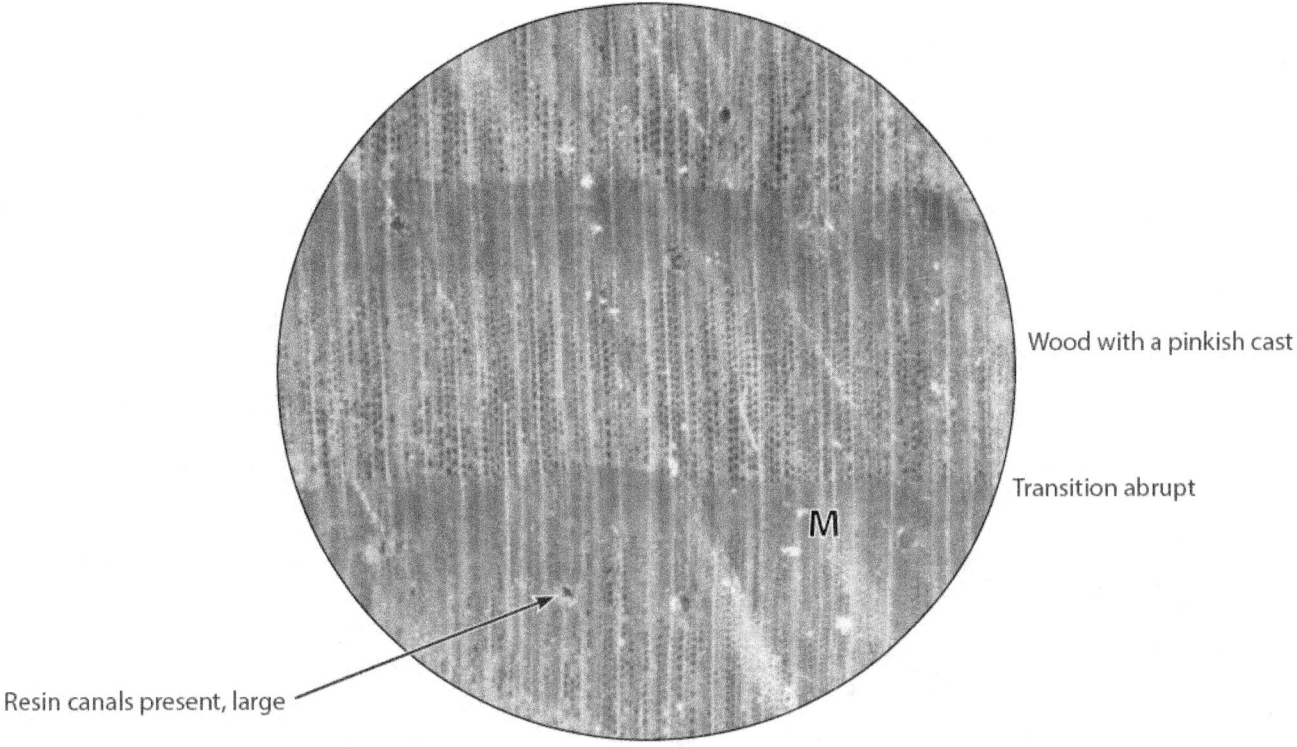

Wood with a pinkish cast

Transition abrupt

Resin canals present, large

National Design Specification guidance

Use the NDS Red Pine designation for timber-size members, but the Spruce–Pine–Fir designation is recommended for dimension lumber.

Notes

Yellow Pine Group (not Southern)

Pinus sp., Yellow pine group

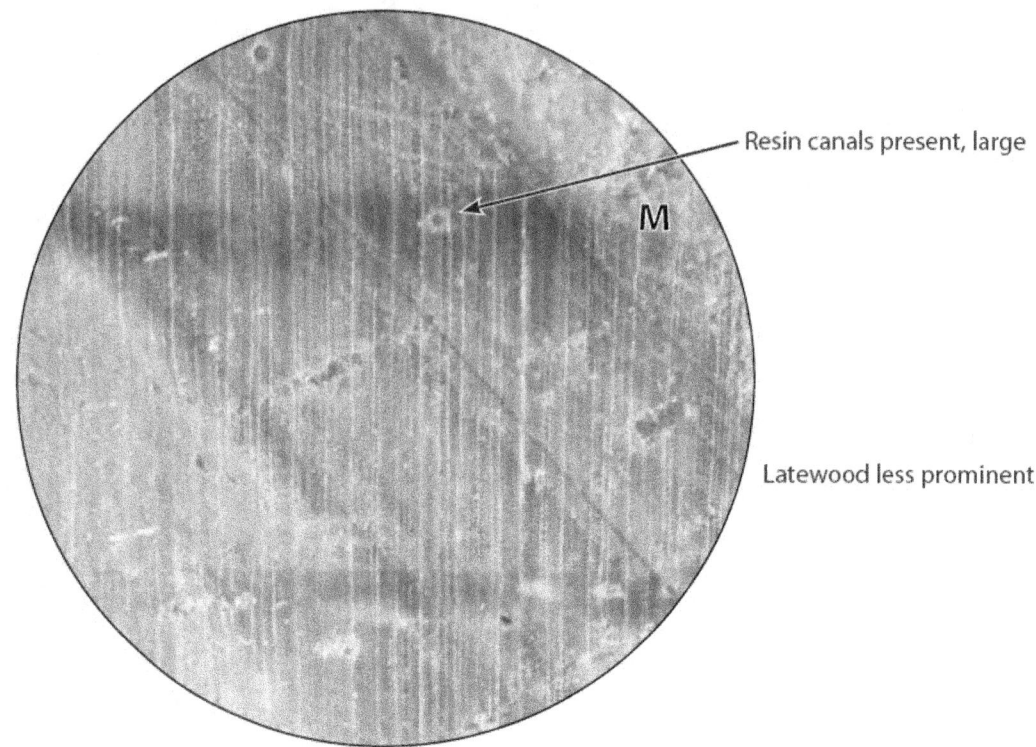

Resin canals present, large

M

Latewood less prominent

National Design Specification guidance

Use the Spruce–Pine–Fir designation.

Notes

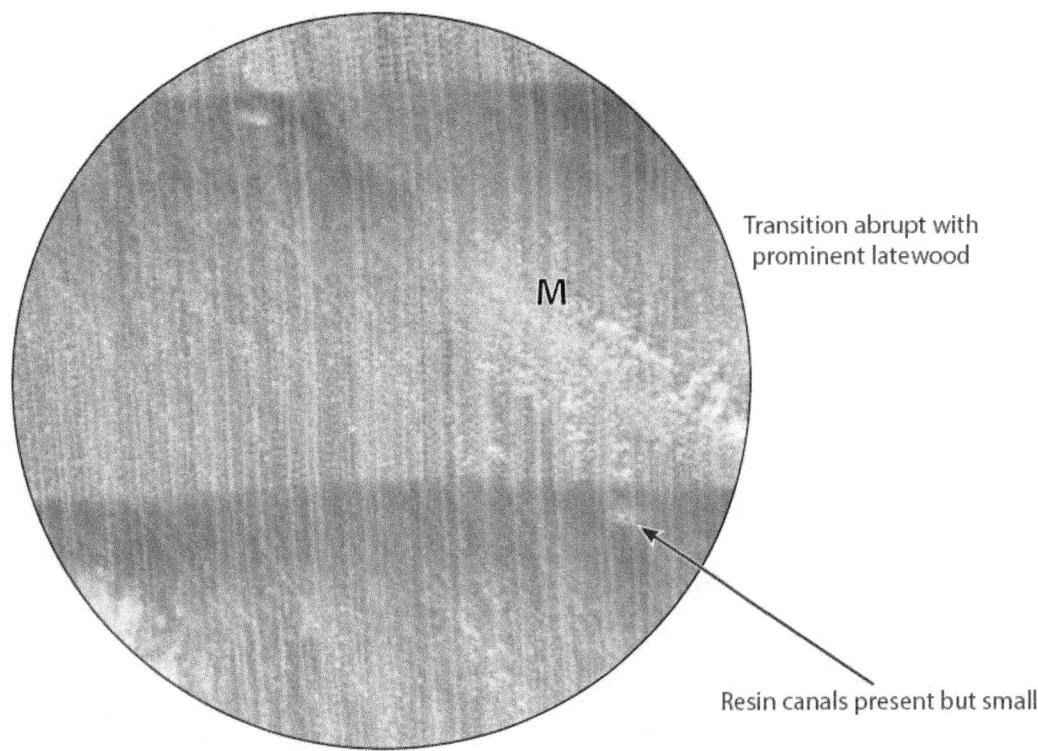

Transition abrupt with prominent latewood

M

Resin canals present but small

National Design Specification guidance

Use the Douglas Fir–Larch designation if known to be Western Larch, otherwise use the Eastern Hemlock–Tamarack designation.

Notes

Douglas-fir

Pseudotsuga cf. *mensiezii*

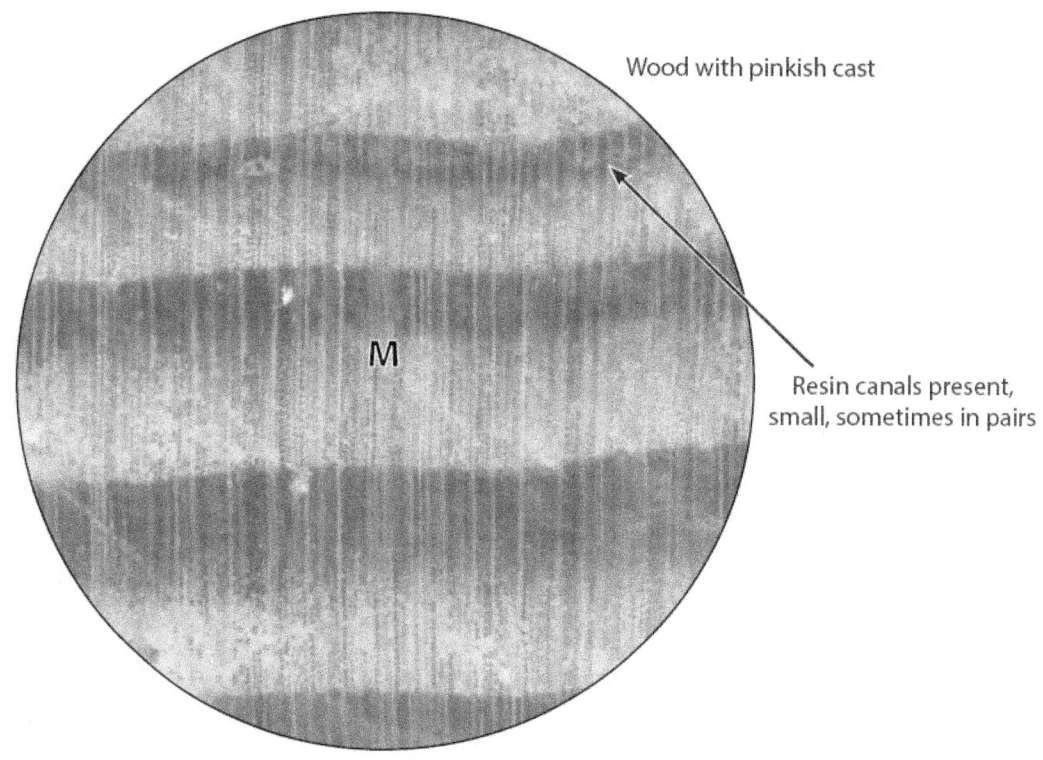

Wood with pinkish cast

Resin canals present, small, sometimes in pairs

National Design Specification guidance

Use the Douglas Fir–Larch designation. The geographic origin of the material, if known, will determine whether to use the North or South category. If unknown, use the lower of the two values.

Notes

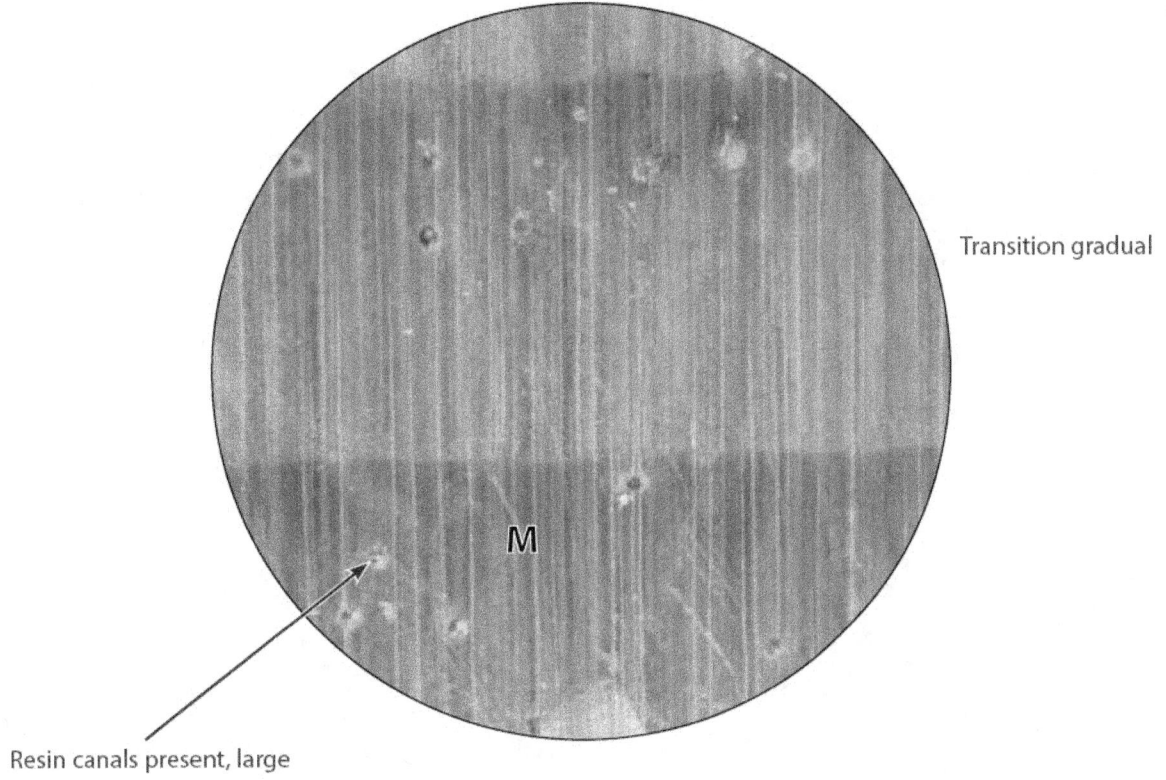

Transition gradual

M

Resin canals present, large

National Design Specification guidance

If wood is of Eastern U.S. origin, use the Eastern White Pine values. If wood is of Western U.S. origin, use the Spruce–Pine–Fir designation.

Notes

Spruce

Picea sp.

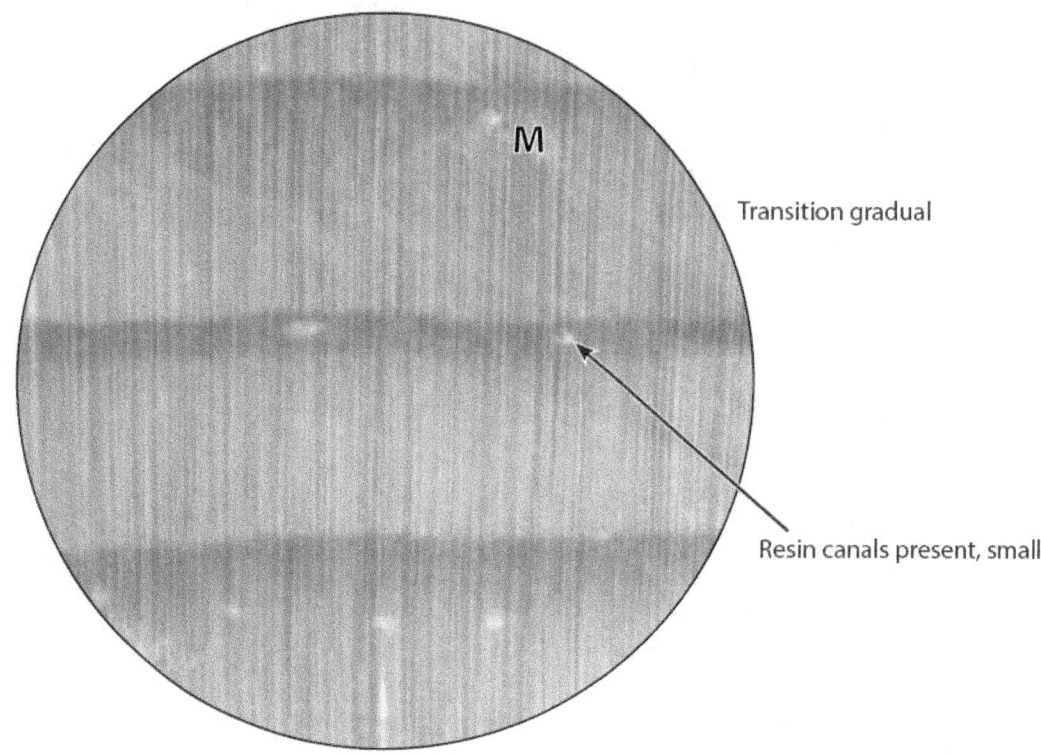

M

Transition gradual

Resin canals present, small

National Design Specification guidance

Use the Spruce–Pine–Fir designation.

Notes

Baldcypress

Taxodium distichum

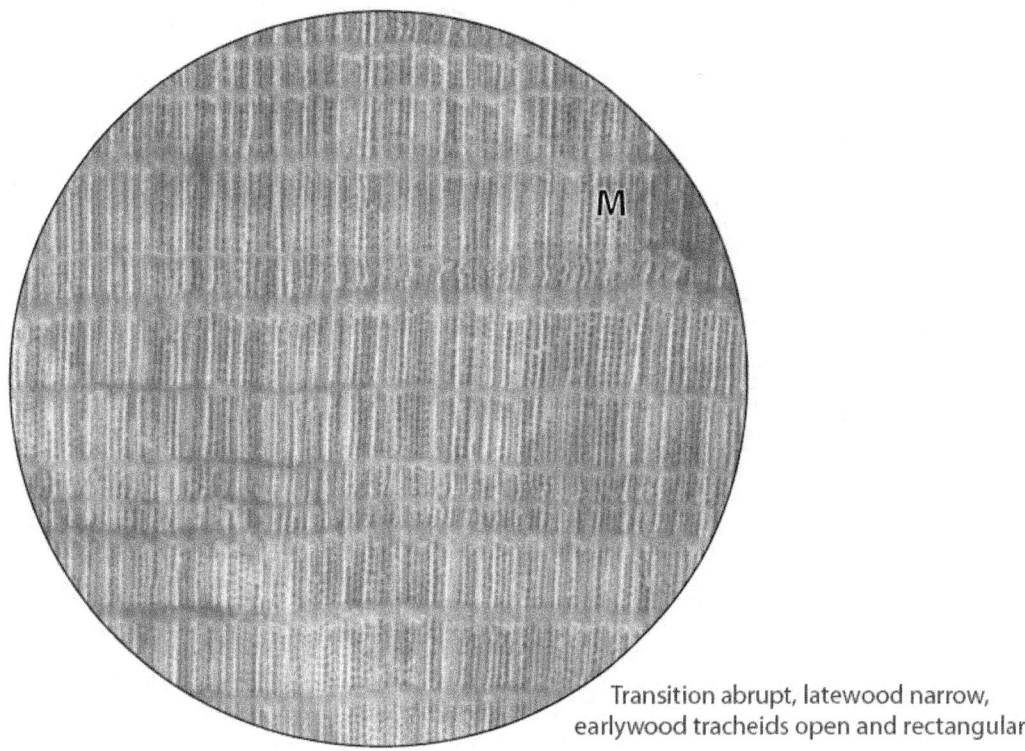

Transition abrupt, latewood narrow,
earlywood tracheids open and rectangular

National Design Specification guidance

Use the Baldcypress designation.

Notes

Redwood

Sequoia/Sequoiadendron sp.

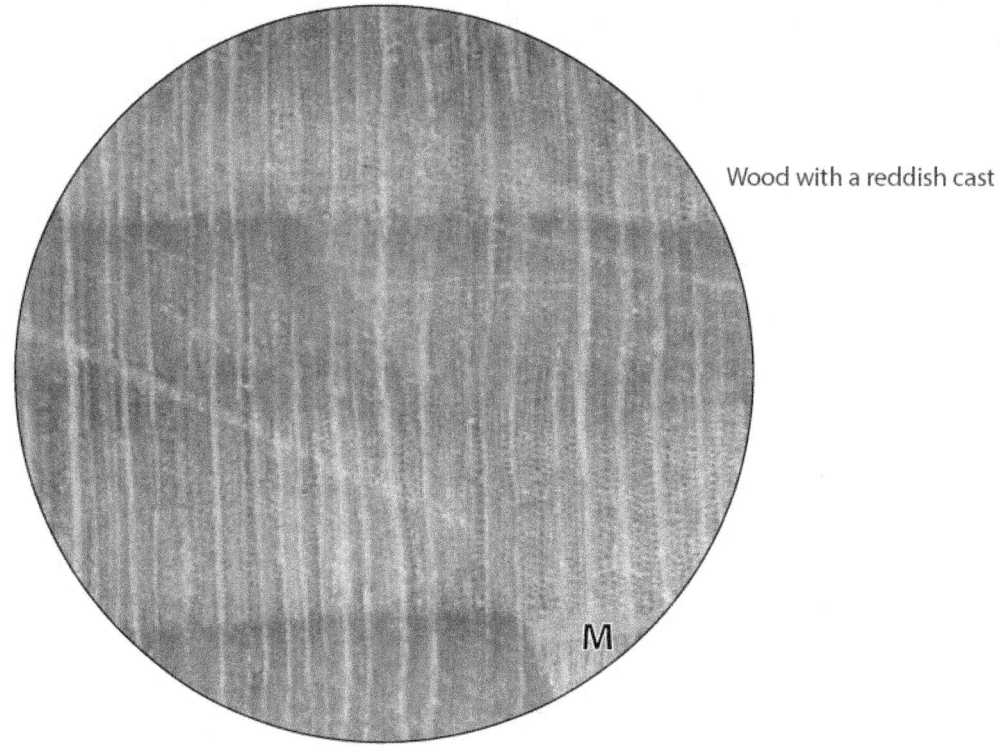

Wood with a reddish cast

National Design Specification guidance

Use the Redwood designation.

Notes

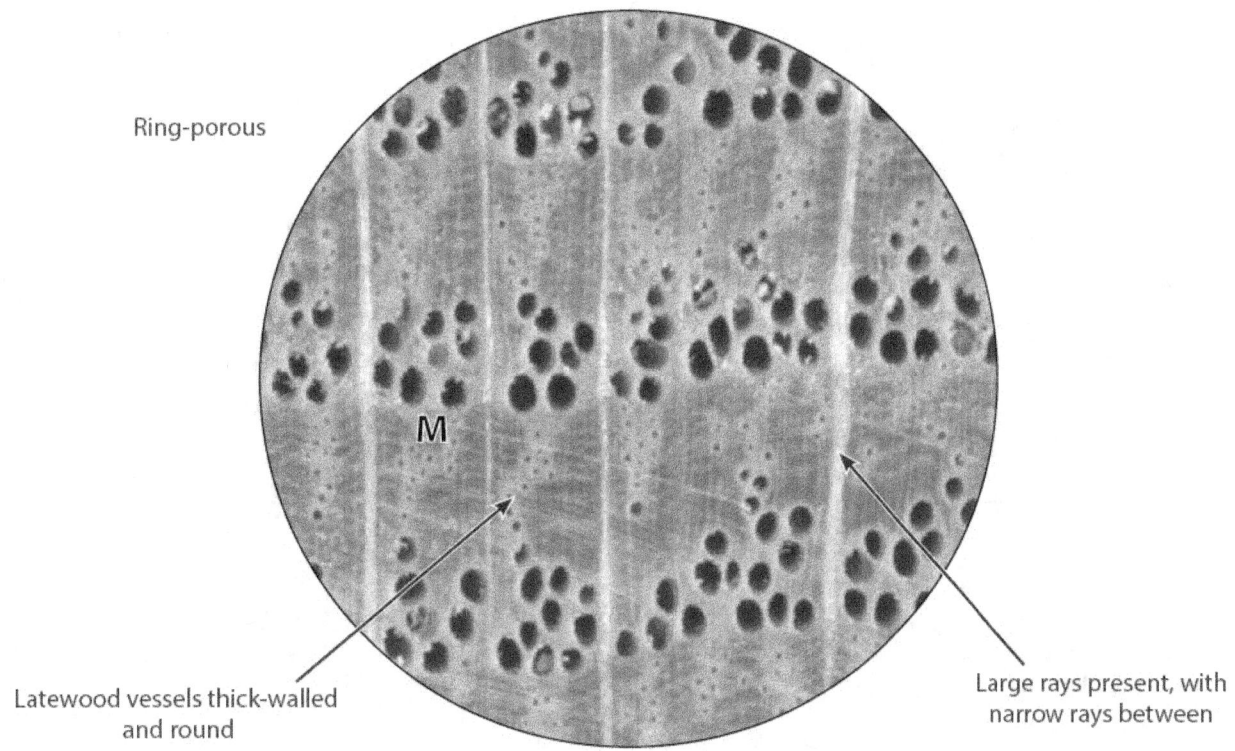

Ring-porous

M

Latewood vessels thick-walled
and round

Large rays present, with
narrow rays between

National Design Specification guidance

Use the geographic origin of the timber, if known, to determine whether to use the Northern or Southern values for Red Oak. If origin is unknown, use the lower values.

Notes

White Oak Group

Quercus sp., white oak group

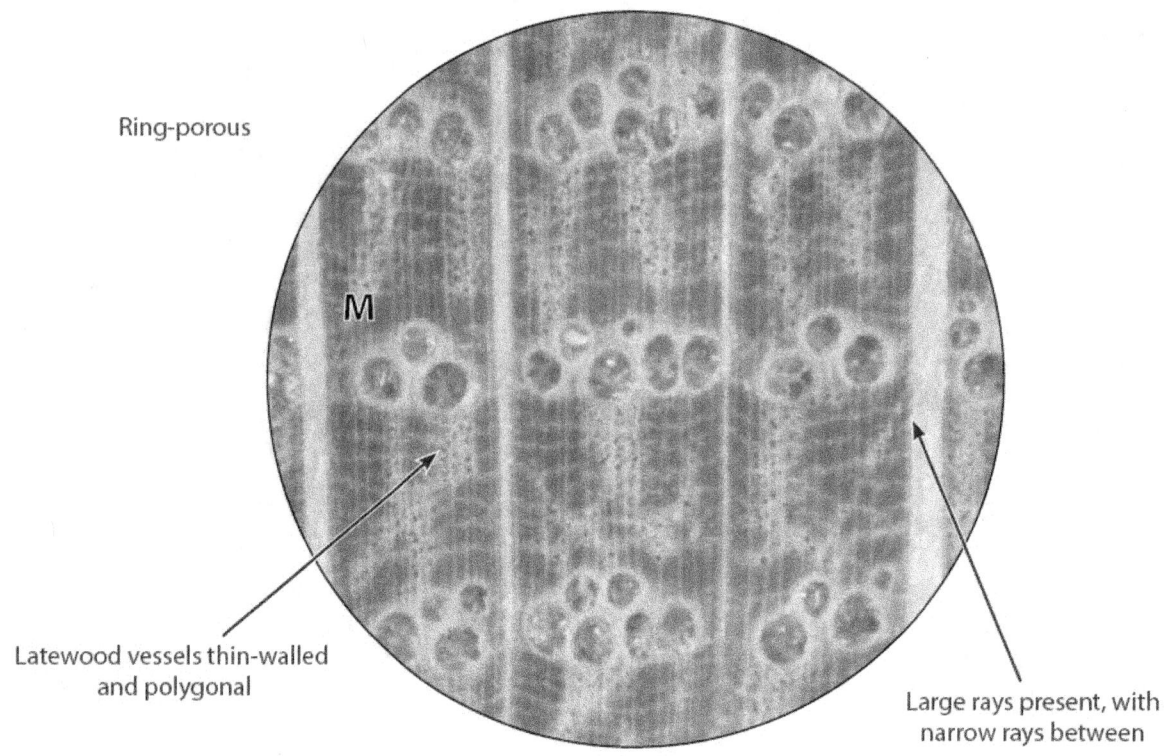

Ring-porous

M

Latewood vessels thin-walled
and polygonal

Large rays present, with
narrow rays between

National Design Specification guidance

Use the White Oak Group designation.

Notes

Elm or Hackberry

Ulmus sp. or *Celtis* sp.

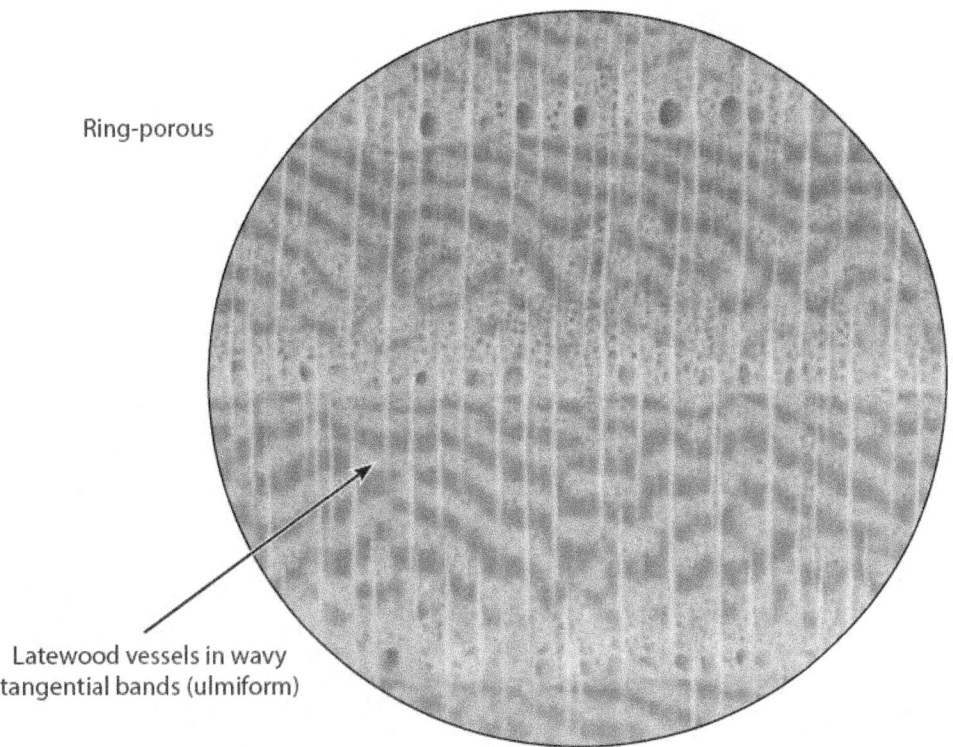

Ring-porous

Latewood vessels in wavy
tangential bands (ulmiform)

National Design Specification guidance

These species are currently not in the NDS specifications, so you will need to make a clear wood estimate.

Notes

Hickory or Pecan

Carya sp.

Ring-porous

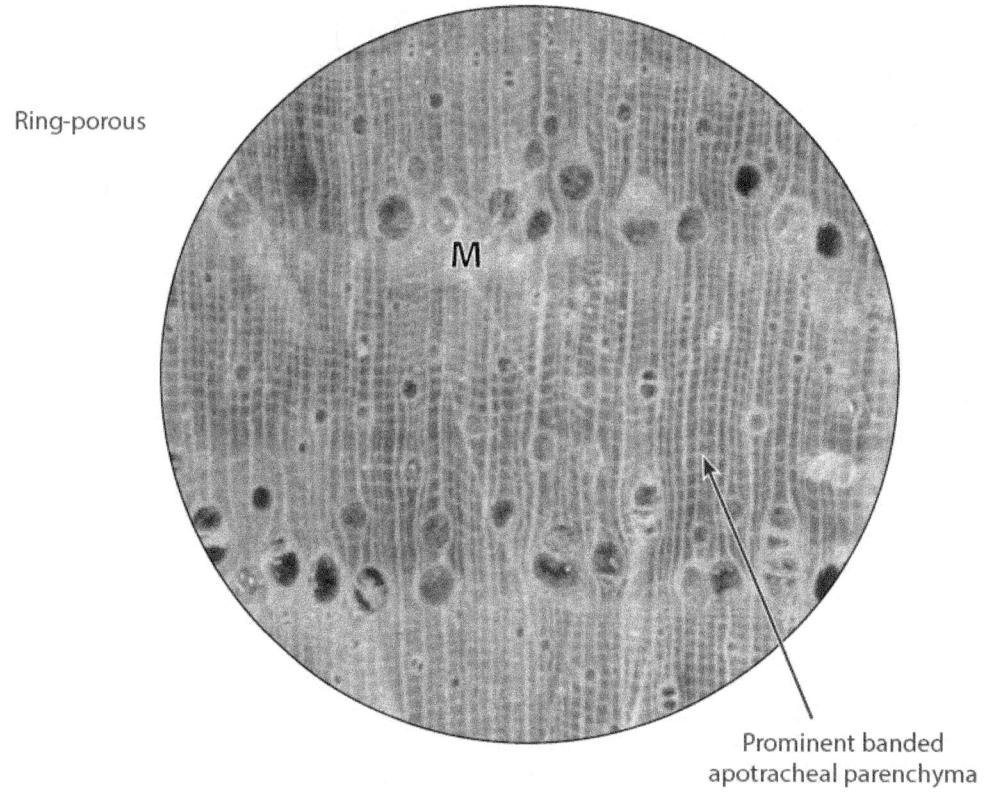

M

Prominent banded
apotracheal parenchyma

National Design Specification guidance

Use the Beech–Birch–Hickory designation.

Notes

Walnut or Butternut

Juglans sp.

Semi-ring-porous

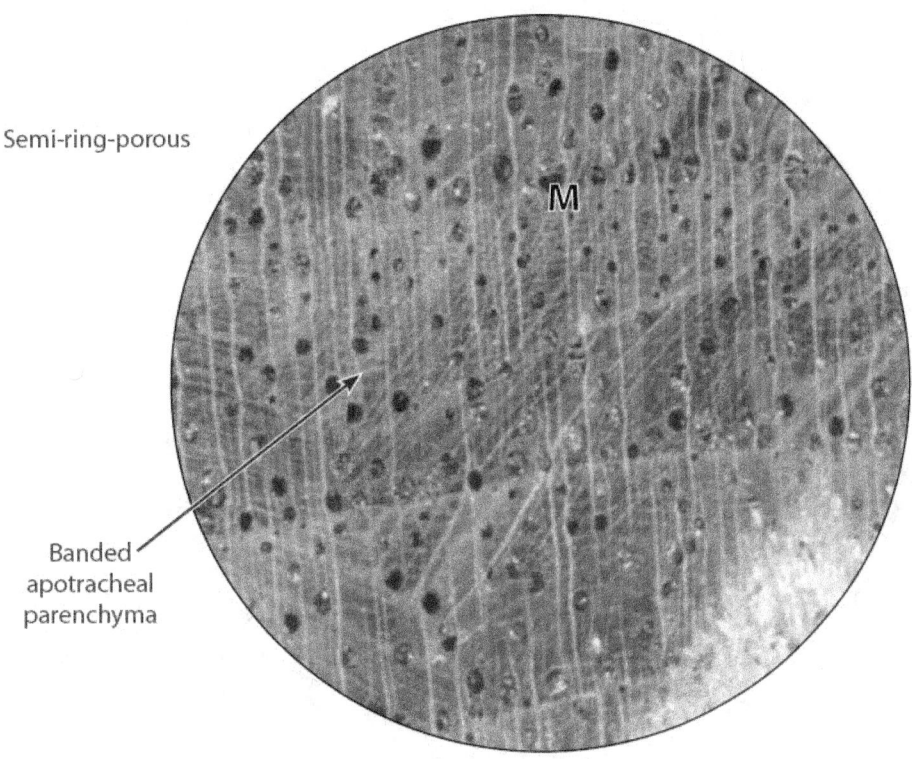

M

Banded
apotracheal
parenchyma

National Design Specification guidance

This species is currently not in the NDS specifications, so you will need to make a clear wood estimate.

Notes

Ash

Fraxinus sp.

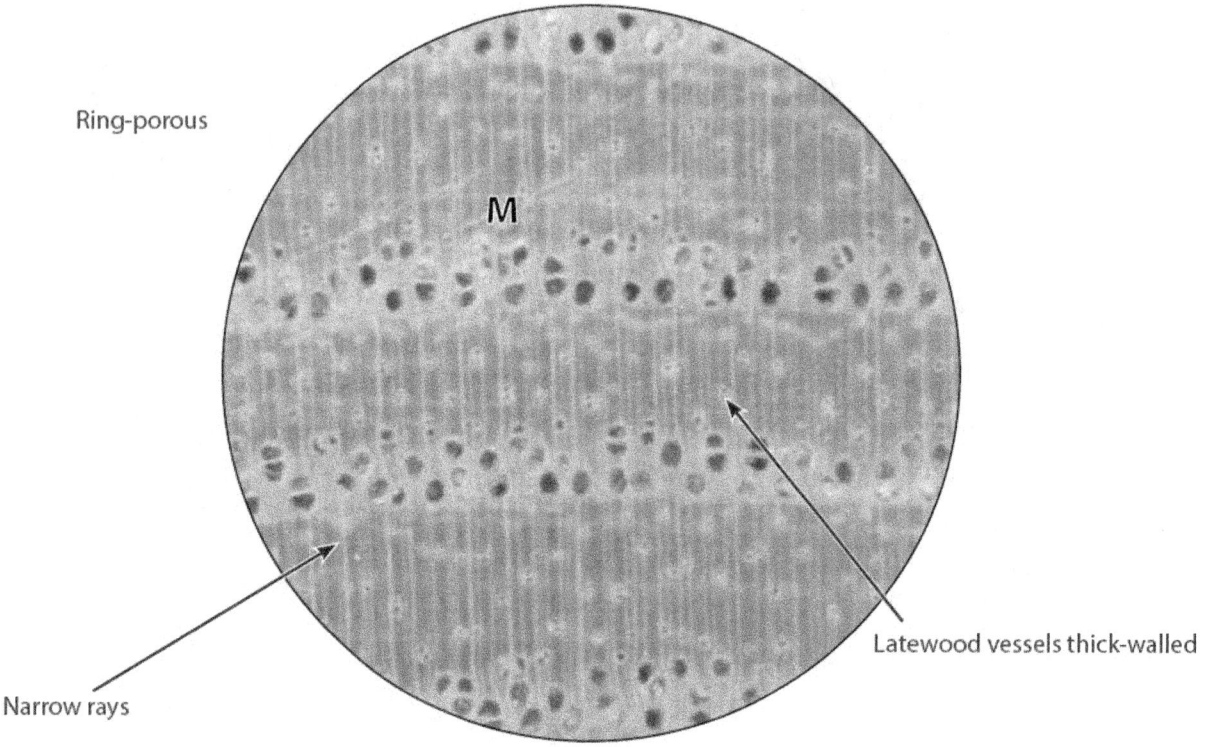

Ring-porous

M

Latewood vessels thick-walled

Narrow rays

National Design Specification guidance

This species is currently not in the NDS specifications, so you will need to make a clear wood estimate.

Notes

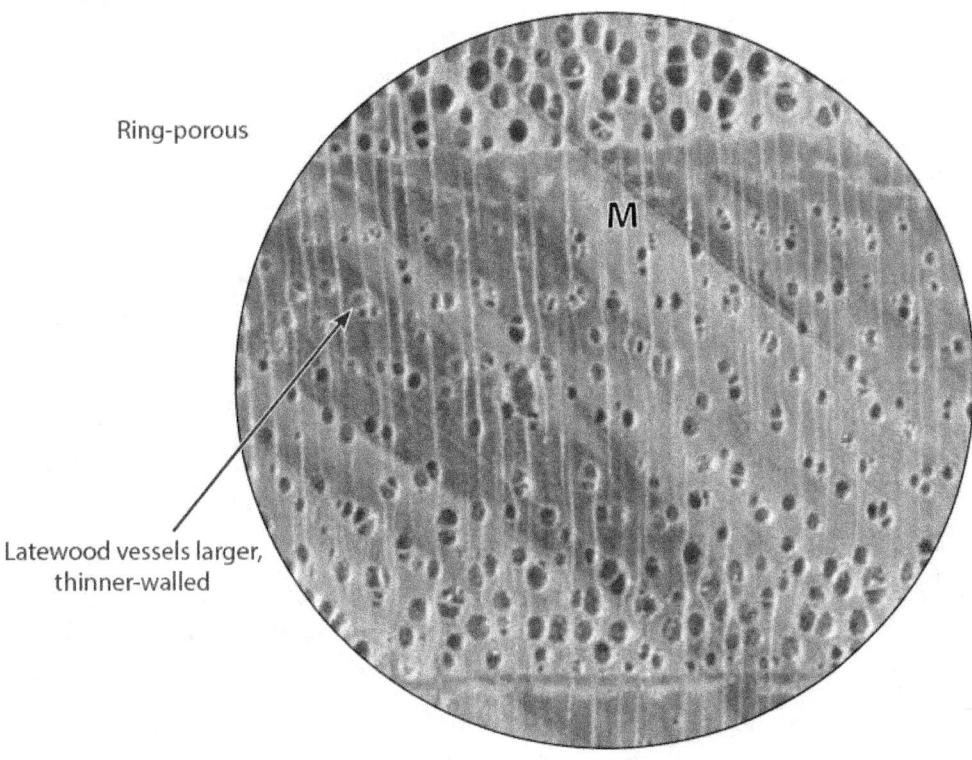

Ring-porous

M

Latewood vessels larger,
thinner-walled

National Design Specification guidance

This species is currently not in the NDS specifications, so you will need to make a clear wood estimate.

Notes

Chestnut

Castanea sp.

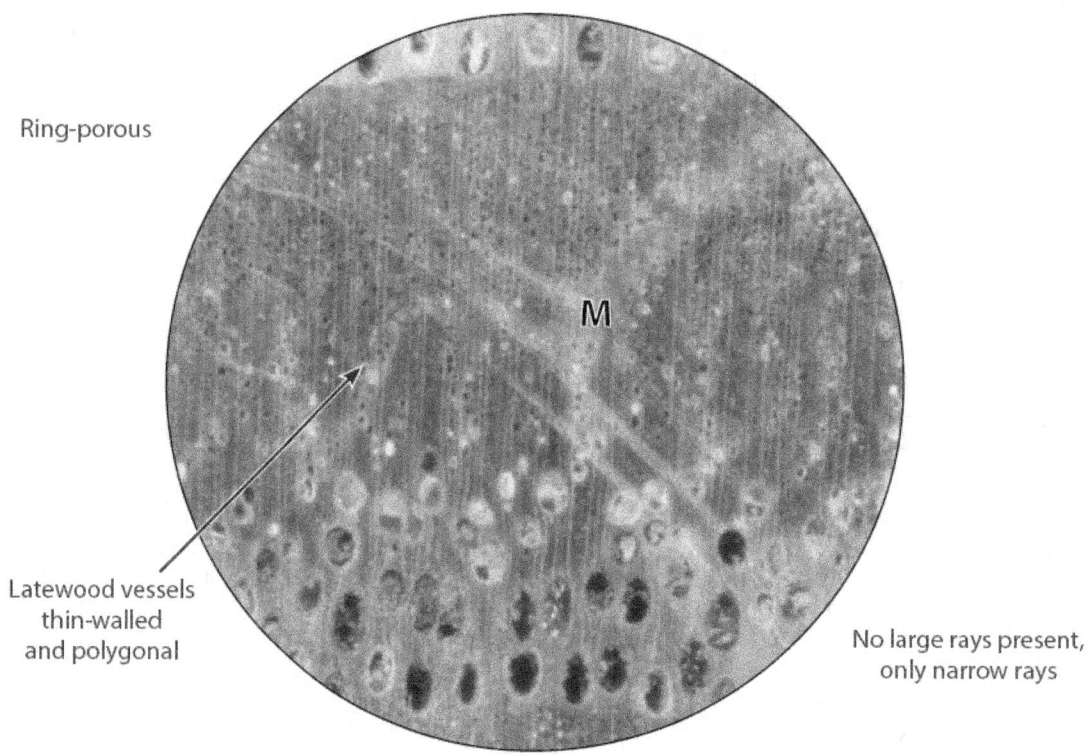

Ring-porous

M

Latewood vessels
thin-walled
and polygonal

No large rays present,
only narrow rays

National Design Specification guidance

This species is currently not in the NDS specifications, so you will need to make a clear wood estimate.

Notes

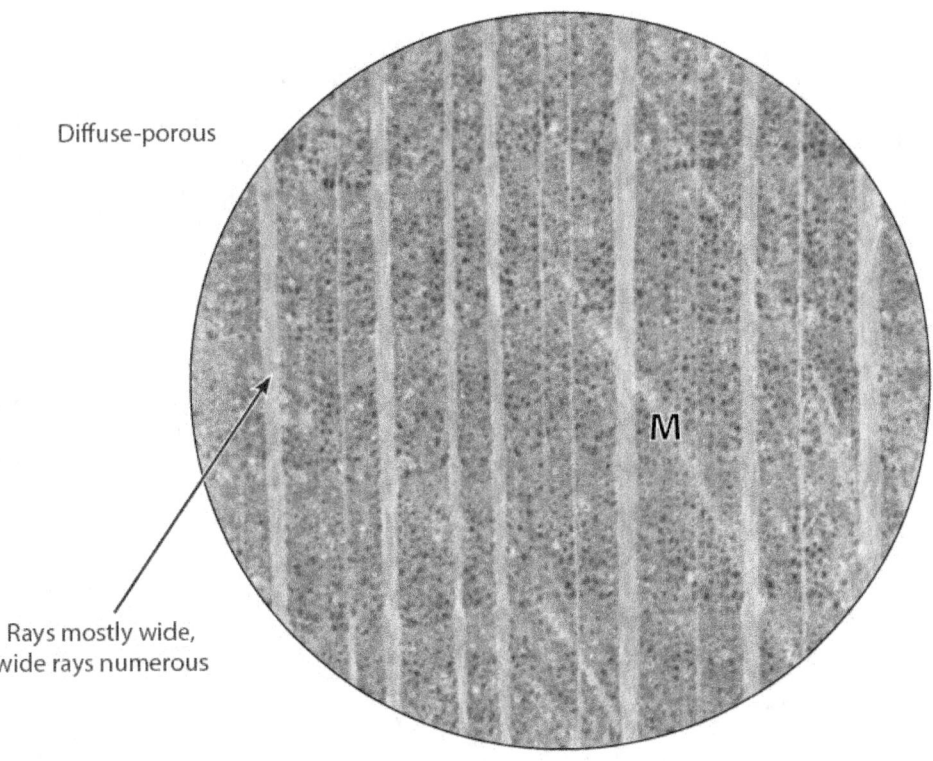

Diffuse-porous

M

Rays mostly wide,
wide rays numerous

National Design Specification guidance

This species is currently not in the NDS specifications, so you will need to make a clear wood estimate.

Notes

Beech

Fagus grandifolia

Diffuse-porous

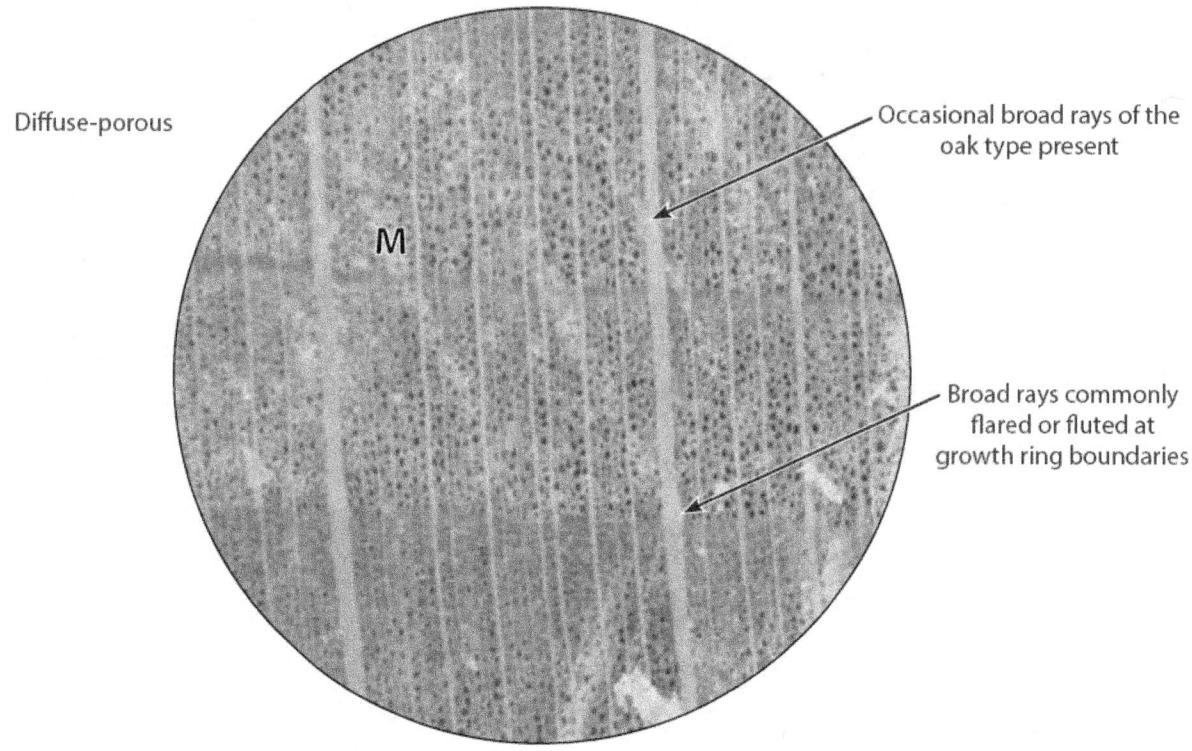

Occasional broad rays of the oak type present

Broad rays commonly flared or fluted at growth ring boundaries

National Design Specification guidance

Use the Beech–Birch–Hickory designation.

Notes

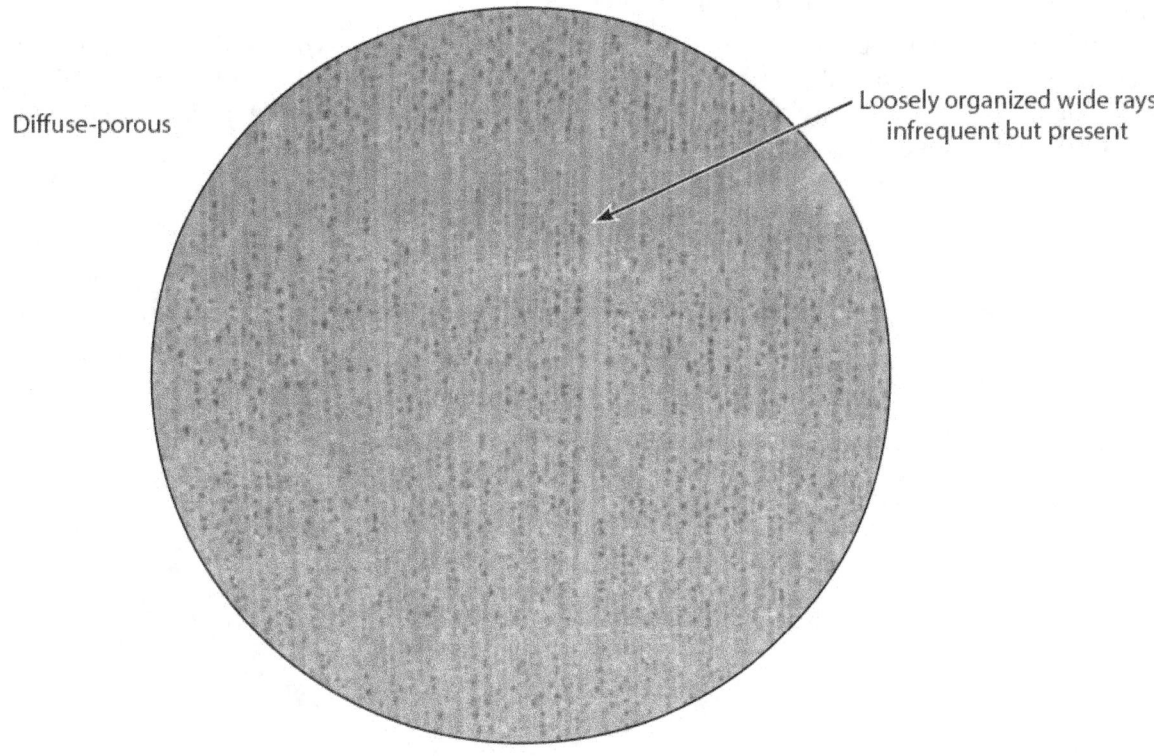

Diffuse-porous

Loosely organized wide rays
infrequent but present

National Design Specification guidance

This species is currently not in the NDS specifications, so you will need to make a clear wood estimate.

Notes

Unrecognized Hardwood

National Design Specification guidance

No useful guidance can be given for estimating strength properties of the wood without further identification of the wood itself. Removing a small specimen (1/4 in. square across the grain and 1–2 in. along the grain) and submitting it to an extension forester or forest products specialist should provide the necessary information to allow further estimation of properties.

Notes

Diffuse-porous

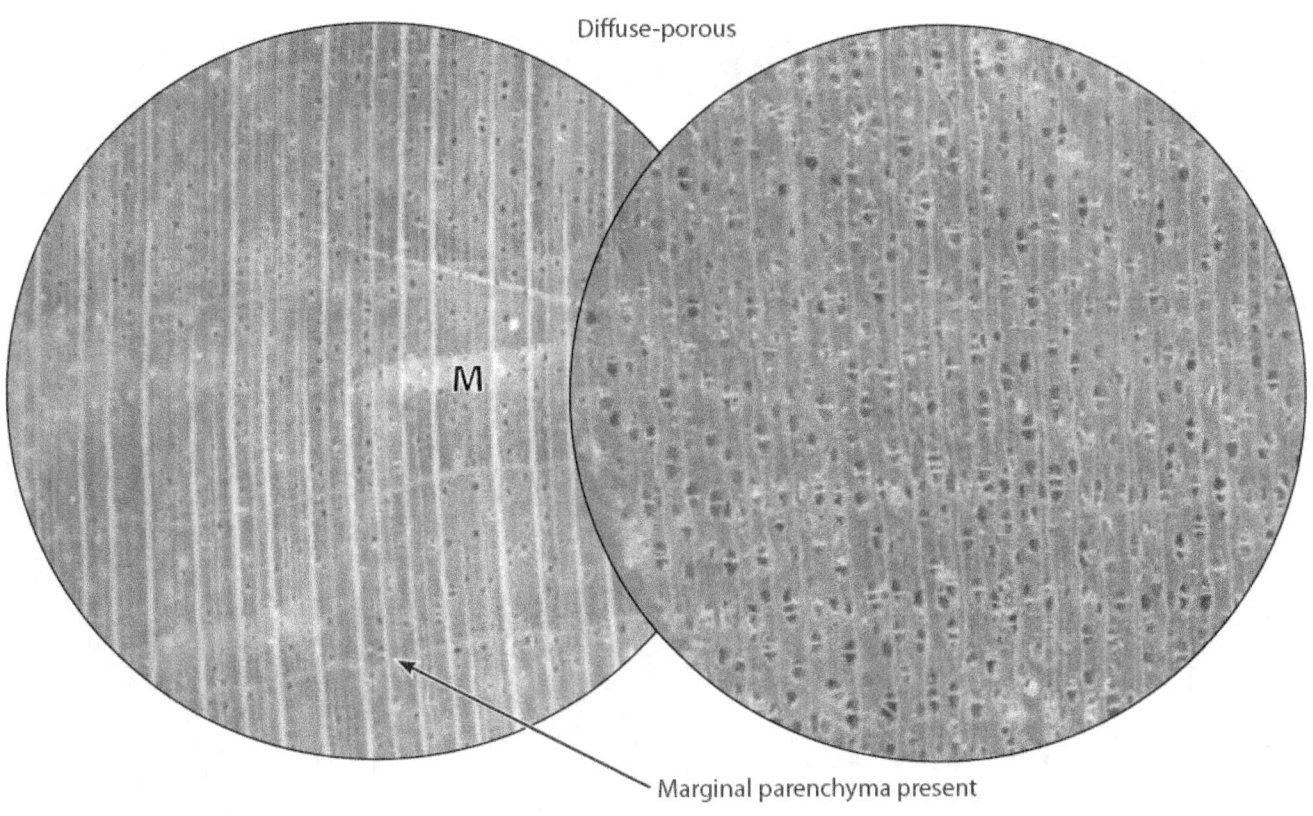

M

Marginal parenchyma present

National Design Specification guidance
Use the Beech–Birch–Hickory designation.

Notes

Yellow Poplar or Magnolia

Liriodendron tulipifera or *Magnolia* sp.

Diffuse-porous

Wood with greenish or purplish cast and luster

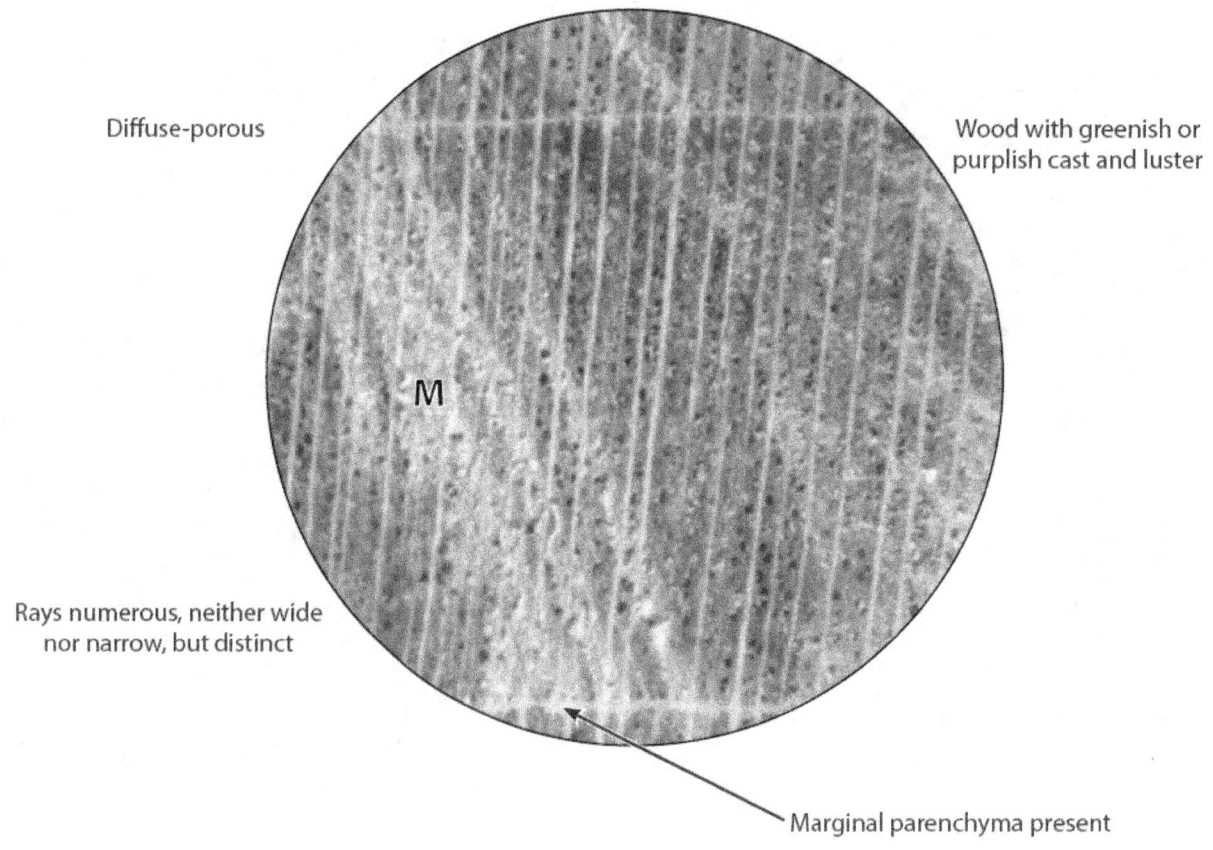

M

Rays numerous, neither wide nor narrow, but distinct

Marginal parenchyma present

National Design Specification guidance

Use the Yellow Poplar designation.

Notes

Basswood

Tilia sp.

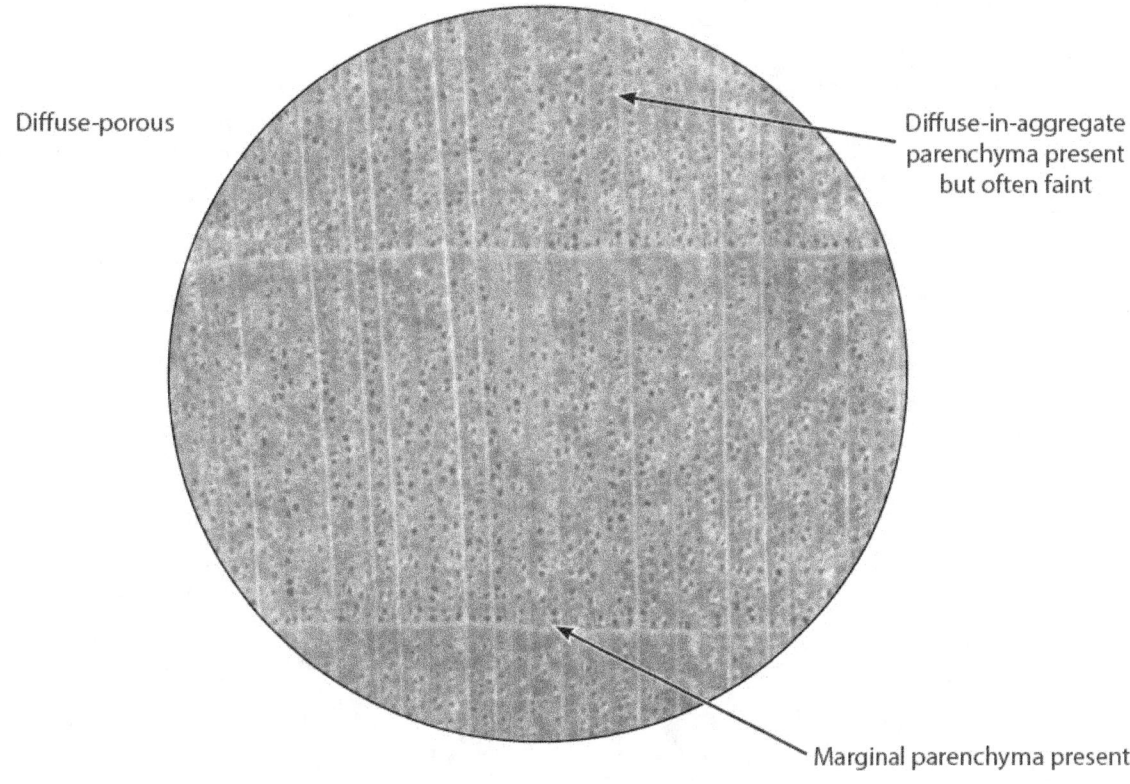

Diffuse-porous

Diffuse-in-aggregate parenchyma present but often faint

Marginal parenchyma present

National Design Specification guidance

This species is currently not in the NDS specifications, so you will need to make a clear wood estimate.

Notes

Aspen/Poplar/Cottonwood

Populus sp.

Diffuse-porous

Vessels abundant, rays extremely
narrow and abundant

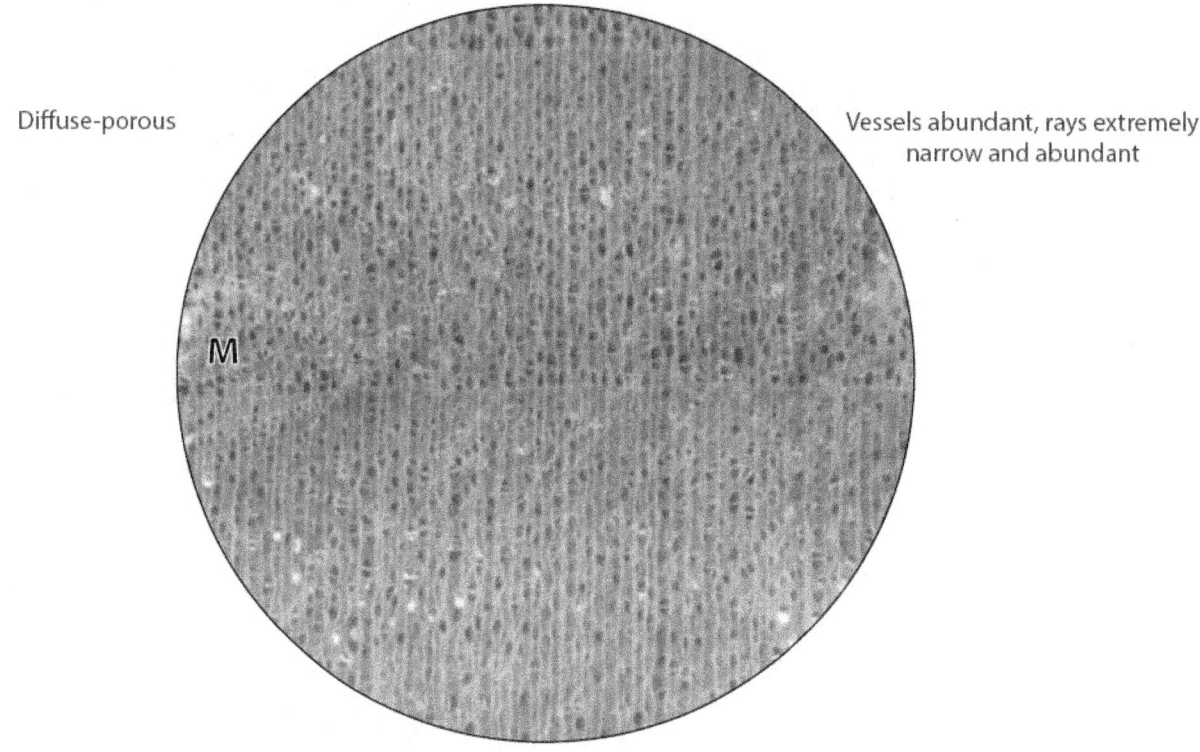

National Design Specification guidance

Use the Aspen or Cottonwood designations if the origin of the material is known. Western or far Northern woods are likely to be Aspen. Eastern or more Southern woods are likely to be Cottonwood.

Notes

8 | Additional information about wood identification

8.1 The limits of wood identification

In using the key and the species description pages, we are sure you noticed that identification of an exact species is rarely possible. This is due in part to the nature of the tools we are using in this manual. A hand lens is a powerful tool for wood identification, but it is not the most powerful method for identification based on anatomical characteristics. The greatest power in wood identification comes with the use of light microscopy in a laboratory with a scientifically valid reference collection (more about reference collections below). Even in such a setting and with a microscope, species-level identification is still not possible by wood anatomy in most cases.

This limit, and it is a profound one, is not a result of a lack of effort on the part of wood anatomy researchers, but rather reflects a basic biological truth; species are defined by flowers, fruits, leaves, and other external characteristics. Internal characteristics, like wood anatomy, often do not vary from one species to another in the same genus, and so species cannot be separated using them. At the time of this writing, there are a number of efforts around the world to use other scientific techniques to identify exact species of wood, and in some cases, to match a specific log, board, or wood product to a stump left behind in the field. Most of these methods depend on either DNA technology or sophisticated techniques in chemistry or spectroscopy. To date none of these techniques have proved universally reliable and are still costly and time-consuming, and are considered experimental. If and when the day arrives that a technological solution is available to ensure species identification of wood, it is not likely to be equally available in all countries and regions and will probably involve laboratory rather than field analysis.

8.2 Additional wood identification information

Many wood identification references are available in addition to this manual. Many of them are written for professional wood anatomists with specific emphasis on the microscopic identification of wood. These resources, though parts will exceed your current knowledge, may nonetheless prove useful in your work. Other references will be more appropriate for your use as you develop your skills in wood identification. It is important to keep in mind that not all references are of the same quality; some references, even well-known ones, have significant flaws or errors. Below we list a small selection of resources, as well as some candid comments about the reliability of the information in each.

InsideWood

InsideWood. 2004 onwards. Published on the Internet. North Carolina State University, Raleigh, NC. (http://insidewood.lib.ncsu.edu/search?2)
This is a tremendously useful resource for wood identification in the laboratory, with a distinct emphasis on light microscopic identification. It incorporates a (usually) complete anatomical characterization of each species in the database, allows rapid searching, and many of the species it covers are illustrated with a variety of photographs. Despite the emphasis on microscopy, many of the species in the database have one or more images similar in magnification to those in this manual. InsideWood is being updated, improved, and maintained regularly as of this writing, so it continues to improve as a resource.

Hoadley's books

Hoadley, R.B. 2000. *Understanding Wood: A Craftsman's Guide to Wood Technology.* 2nd Ed. Newtown, CT: Taunton Press.
Hoadley, R.B. 1990. *Identifying Wood: Accurate Results with Simple Tools.* Newtown, CT: Taunton Press.
These books provide basic information on the structure, properties, and identification of woods, with a greater emphasis on North American species. The information is clearly presented with high-quality illustrations, but emphasizes microscopic rather than hand lens observation of wood for identification.

Textbook of Wood Technology

Panshin, A.J. and C. deZeeuw. 1980. *Textbook of Wood Technology.* 4th Ed. New York: McGraw-Hill.
This is a famous but out-of-print college textbook for understanding many aspects of wood technology, including detailed information on wood identification of North American species. The identification keys in the book are of questionable consistency and reliability. Despite the comparative weakness of the keys themselves, the earlier chapters reviewing the scientific literature in wood technology are useful and relatively up-to-date as of the year of publication.

9 | Estimation of size and grade of members

An inspecting engineer must take three critical steps in order to assign the most accurate estimate of design values to wood members in a bridge: (1) identify the species of wood, (2) estimate a size and grade for the member (Fig. 9.1), and (3) determine the condition of the wood in the member.

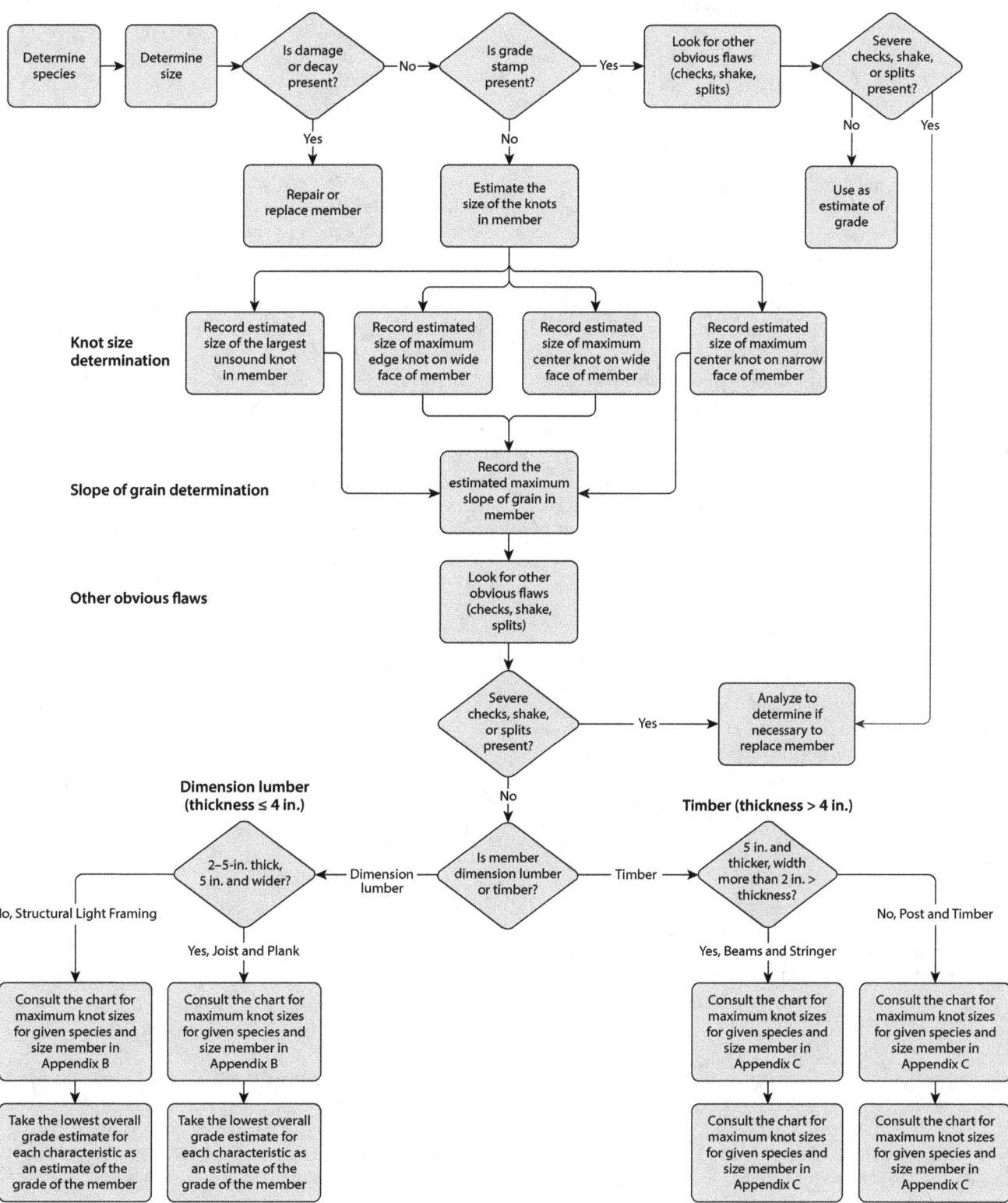

Figure 9.1—Steps for member grading.

9.1 Significance of species

The first and probably most critical step is for the species of the member to be identified. Wood properties for clear wood vary considerably from species to species, as illustrated in selected examples in Table 9.1 (FPL 2010). Values reported in Table 9.1 are average measured properties of small clear specimens in a laboratory setting and are not design values. Chapters 5, 6, and 7 detail the features, skills, and characters used to make a field identification of wooden members likely to be found in a timber bridge in the United States.

9.1.1 Sampling of bridge members

The best piece of advice that can be given for sampling bridge members is "have a plan." With photos or hand drawings, establish a system for identifying, cataloging, and recording property estimates for the members. Different species can be used for different sections of the bridge; therefore, the ability to trace the location to positions on the structure is very important. An inspector must also consider which members should be prioritized, which can be accomplished by preliminary structural analysis to save time and effort in the field.

9.1.2 What to prioritize in sampling for wood ID

As is often the case with inspections, limited time and resources are available. The inspector should prioritize the members that are most critical to structural performance of the bridge. The species of wood in these members should be the first to be identified.

9.1.3 How to collect samples for wood ID

Samples can be obtained by coring a member, drilling with a hole saw, or collecting broken splinters. Each sample should be gathered in individual containers and labeled so that samples can be traced back to the members they came from. A large enough sample must be taken so that the techniques explained in Chapter 4 can be safely applied, but it should not be taken in a way that affects structural integrity of the member.

9.1.4 How many samples to take

It may be likely that the same species would be used for most members. However, a sufficient number of samples should be taken to ensure that the species involved in the most critical structural members are thoroughly represented. A minimum of 20% of those members should be sampled for identification. Approximately 10% of the other less critical structural members should also be sampled for identification.

9.2 Size of member

Before an estimated grade can be assigned to a particular member, the size of that member must be accurately estimated. If you are inspecting a bridge that was built or refurbished since 1970, you will be able to directly use much of the information tabulated in the current NIST Product Standard PS 20 related to size (Table 9.2, DOC PS 20, Smith and Wood 1964). Wood members are divided into three categories: boards, dimension lumber, and timbers. Structural members are classified as either dimension lumber or timbers. Most historic bridges, however, were built before the current methods assigning design values to structural wood members were standardized. Sizes of members likely will not be the standard sizes you are accustomed to today.

A piece of "dimension lumber" is any structural lumber that has a nominal thickness of 2 to 4 in. (actual thickness of 38 to 114 mm (1.5 to 4.5 in.)). A piece of "timber" is a structural member that has a nominal thickness greater than 5 in. (actual thickness greater than 114 mm (4.5 in.)). Timbers are further subdivided, based on use, into subcategories of "Beam and Stringer" (timbers used as bending members) and "Post and Timber" (timbers used more as compression and tension members). The size of a member directly influences the capacity of the member and will help determine which design values "dimension lumber or timbers" should be associated with it.

All three dimensions of a lumber member need to be determined (Fig. 9.2). The thickness of a member is the measured dimension of the narrower face of a rectangular piece of lumber. The width of the member is the measured dimension of the larger face of a rectangular piece of lumber. The length of the member is the measured dimension of the largest dimension of the member. Measurement is best accomplished using digital calipers and measuring tapes on exposed cross sections of members. Some more creative means are often required to determine sizes of less accessible members.

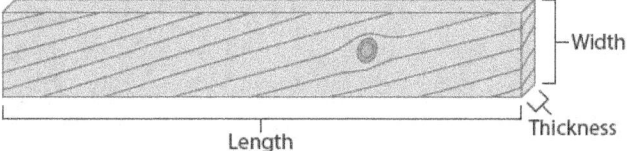

Figure 9.2—Definition of length, width, and thickness in a lumber member.

9.3 Grade of member

An estimate of grade will be required for an inspector to initially estimate design values for a member. Unfortunately, estimating grade for an inspector is an imprecise business that requires a great deal of judgment. The information in this section is meant to provide inspectors with a very basic overview of grading and allow them to make crude judgments on the grade of members. Becoming proficient in visual grading requires many hours of experience. Some basic understanding of the grading process will allow an inspector to judge whether a more thorough grading of members is advised. Experienced certified graders should be hired to provide the truest estimate-of-grade for members.

9.3.1 Purpose of grading

To more efficiently and economically use wood from logs, pieces of wood of similar mechanical properties are placed in categories called stress grades, which are characterized by (a) one or more sorting criteria, (b) a set of properties for engineering design, and (c) a unique grade name. With new material, a grade stamp on a piece of lumber tells architects, engineers, builders, and building officials the quality of a piece of lumber. A typical grade stamp for dimension lumber is shown in Figure 9.3. A grade stamp provides information on the supervising grading agency (WWPA), the wood species or species combination (Douglas Fir–Larch), the mill number or brand of the firm that produced the board (12), the grade requirements the piece meets (No. 1 and better), and the target moisture content to which the wood was dried or the moisture content at which it was surfaced (surfaced-green). If a grade stamp is present, the inspector's job is immediately made easier. A certified grader has already judged the grade of the member based on the most severe defects present. If the inspector determines that the member is still undamaged and undecayed, this grade can be used to determine the design values (Chapter 11). If not, additional judgments on the quality of the member must be made.

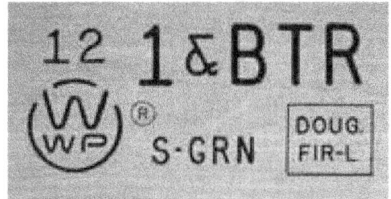

Figure 9.3—Grade stamp from WWPA No. 1 & Better dimension lumber. Moisture content is surfaced green (unseasoned) condition, over 19%.

9.3.2 Brief history of visual grading

For many years, lumber has demonstrated the versatility of wood by serving as a primary raw material for construction and manufacture in the United States. In this role, lumber has been produced in a wide variety of products from many different species. The first industry-sponsored grading rules (product descriptions) for softwoods, which were established before 1900, were comparatively simple because sawmills marketed their lumber locally and grades had only local significance. As new timber sources across the United States were developed and lumber was transported to distant points, each producing region continued to establish its own grading rules. Lumber from various regions differed in size, grade name, and allowable grade characteristics. When different species were graded under different rules and competed in the same markets, confusion and dissatisfaction were inevitable.

Research conducted on wood properties in the early 1900s had two distinct camps: full-size testing and small clear wood testing. The full-size testing group felt that testing programs and any subsequent grading standards should be done on full-size members available to consumers. This group argued that this approach would reduce the waste involved in overbuilt structures and ensure minimum standards for integrity and safety. The small clear wood group, primarily foresters, felt that timber tests should focus on the qualities of trees rather than the potential design uses for lumber. Their group argued that tests of multiple small samples of clear wood should be conducted to provide strength averages without incurring the expenses and waste that full-size testing would generate (Green and Evans 2001). This debate continues to this day.

As grading rules began to develop, a number of conferences were sponsored by the U.S. Department of Commerce from 1919 to 1925 to minimize unnecessary differences in grading rules and to improve and simplify these rules. These conferences were attended by representatives of lumber manufacturers, distributors, wholesalers, retailers, engineers, architects, and contractors. The result of these conferences was a relative standardization of sizes, definitions, and procedures for deriving allowable design properties and a voluntary American Lumber Standard. Two circulars, Circular 295, "Basic Grading Rules and Working Stresses for Structural Timbers," and Circular 296, "Standard Grading Specifications for Yard Lumber," involving allowable design values published by USDA Forest Products Laboratory in 1923, served as the basis for the grading rules we see in the United States today (Newlin and Johnson 1923, Ivory et al. 1923). In the years that followed initial acceptance of the first grading rules, these rules have been modified as more information was gathered on the influence of knots, slope of grain, growth characteristics, and sawing practices.

An orderly, voluntary, but circuitous system of responsibilities has evolved in the United States for the development, manufacture, and merchandizing of most stress-graded lumber (Fig. 9.4). Stress-grading principles are developed from research findings and engineering concepts, often within committees and subcommittees of ASTM International (formerly the American Society for Testing and Materials), and then applied to product classes. Lumber cannot be graded as American Standard lumber unless the grade rules have been approved by the American Lumber Standard Committee (ALSC), Inc., Board of Review. Virtually all commercial softwood and hardwood lumber used for structural purposes that is manufactured in the United States is stress graded under American Lumber Standard practice and is called American Lumber Standard program lumber. The American Lumber Standard has been modified several times, including the addition of hardwood species to the standard beginning in 1970. The current edition is the American Softwood Lumber Standard PS 20–10. Distinctive grade marks for each species or species grouping are provided by accredited agencies. The principles of stress grading are also applied to several hardwood species under provisions of the American Softwood Lumber Standard,

ASTM International, and then applied to product classes. The allowable design properties are tabulated in the Supplement to the National Design Specification (ANSI/AWC NDS; Current Edition).

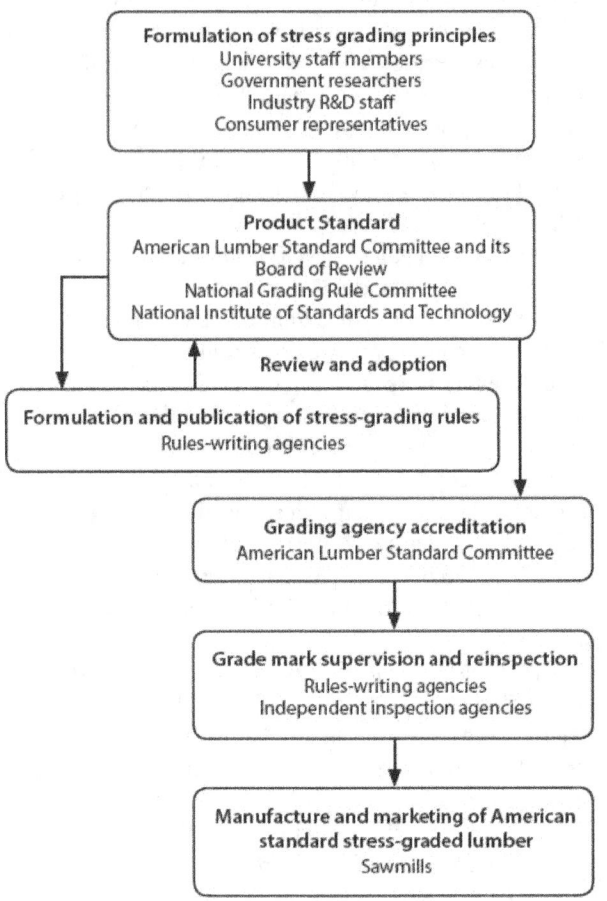

Figure 9.4—Voluntary system of responsibilities for stress grading under the American Softwood Lumber Standard.

Responsibilities and standards for stress grading

Organizations that write and publish grading rule books containing stress-grade descriptions are called rules-writing agencies. Grading rules that specify American Softwood Lumber Standard (ALSC) PS 20 must be certified by the ALSC Board of Review for conformance with this standard. Organizations that write grading rules, as well as independent agencies, can be accredited by the ALSC Board of Review to provide grading and grade-marking supervision and re-inspection services to individual lumber manufacturers. Accredited rules-writing and independent agencies are listed below. These agencies are in the business of grading and have a wealth of experience of determining grades of lumber. The continued accreditation of these organizations is under the scrutiny of the ALSC Board of Review. For the most accurate assessment of grade of a member an accredited grader from one of these organizations should be used.

Tables 9.3, 9.4, and 9.5 provide example grading rules for various grades at the time of this publication. The most current rules for visually grading lumber and timber members can be obtained from various rules-writing agencies that are responsible for supervising lumber mill grading operations. The most up-to-date set of rules can be obtained from the rules-writing agencies. These rules can provide an inspector with a clear guide as to what is acceptable under current visual grading rules.

9.3.3 Current visual grading system

The grading rules in use today, like those discussed in 1923, are based on the premise that mechanical properties of lumber and timbers differ from mechanical properties of clear wood because many growth characteristics affect properties and these characteristics can be seen and judged by eye. The typical visual sorting criteria used in grading are size of member, knots, slope of grain, checks and splits, shake, density, decay, heartwood and sapwood, pitch pockets, and wane.

For dimension lumber (lumber less than 90 mm (nominal 4 in.)), a single set of grade names and descriptions is used throughout the United States, although the design values vary with species. The current National Grading Rule restrictions for dimension lumber are given in Table 9.3.

Timbers (lumber standard 114 mm (nominal 5 in.) or more in least dimension) are also structurally graded under

Sawn lumber grading agencies*

Rules-writing agencies

Northeastern Lumber Manufacturers Association (NeLMA)

Northern Softwood Lumber Bureau (NSLB)

Redwood Inspection Service (RIS)

Southern Pine Inspection Bureau (SPIB)

West Coast Lumber Inspection Bureau (WCLIB)

Western Wood Products Association (WWPA)

National Lumber Grades Authority (NLGA)

Independent agencies

American Institute of Timber Construction

Continental Inspection Agency, LLC

Pacific Lumber Inspection Bureau, Inc.

Stafford Inspection and Consulting, LLC

Renewable Resource Associates, Inc.

Timber Products Inspection

Alberta Forest Products Association

Canadian Lumbermen's Association

Canadian Mill Services Association

Canadian Softwood Inspection Agency, Inc.

Central Forest Products Association

Council of Forest Industries

MacDonald Inspection

Maritime Lumber Bureau

Newfoundland and Labrador Lumber Producers Association

Quebec Forest Industry Council

*For updated information, contact American Lumber Standard Committee, P.O. Box 210, Germantown, MD 20875; alsc@alsc.org; www.alsc.org.

ALSC procedures. Unlike grade descriptions for dimension lumber, grade descriptions for structural timbers are not standardized across species. Structural timbers of Southern Pine are graded without regard to anticipated use (Table 9.4). For most species, however, timber grades are classified according to intended use (Table 9.5).

9.3.4 Influence of visual grading characteristics on grade

Visual grading characteristics influence wood properties and performance, and as such are used as sorting criteria. Such characteristics include knots, slope of grain, checks and splits, shake, density, decay, heartwood and sapwood, pitch pockets, and wane. To make the most exact estimate of a bridge member's grade, all these characteristics should be considered, but the grade of the member will be determined by the most severe of the defects. Not all these member characteristics in a bridge will be easy or possible to measure in place, but their influence on properties is discussed for completeness. The most critical of these characteristics for bridge inspections are highlighted in Section 9.4. With some experience, you will be able identify which of the features explained below represent the most significant or severe defect in the member and only measure that feature.

Knots

Knots are branches or portions of branches embedded in a piece of wood and cause localized cross grain with steep slopes within the timber. A very damaging aspect of knots in sawn lumber is that the continuity of the grain around the knot is interrupted by the sawing process. The location of a knot influences the knot's effect on strength. Centerline knots on the wide face have the least effect on strength grade. Edge knots on the wide or narrow face have the most effect on strength and grade.

In general, knots have greater effect on strength in tension than compression; in bending, the effect depends on whether a knot is in the tension or compression side of a beam (knots along the centerline have little or no effect). Intergrown (or live) knots resist (or transmit) some kinds of stress, but encased knots (unless very tight) or knotholes resist (or transmit) little or no stress. On the other hand, distortion of grain is greater around an intergrown knot than around an encased (or dead) knot of equivalent size. As a result, overall strength effects are roughly equalized, and often no distinction is made in stress grading between intergrown knots, dead knots, and knotholes.

The presence of a knot has a greater effect on most strength properties than on stiffness. The zone of distorted grain (cross grain) around a knot has less "parallel to piece" stiffness than does straight-grained wood; thus, localized areas of low stiffness are often associated with knots. However, such zones generally constitute only a minor part of the total volume of a piece of lumber. Because overall stiffness of a piece reflects the character of all parts, stiffness is not greatly influenced by knots.

Measuring knots

It is important to know the size and location of knots in wood members of a timber bridge. The effect of knots on strength depends approximately on the proportion of the cross section of the piece of lumber occupied by the knot, knot location, and distribution of stress in the member. Grading criteria thus place limits on knot sizes in relation to the width of the face and location on the face in which the knot appears (Fig. 9.5), and the influence of the worst or most severe knot determines whether the knot is the limiting factor for determining the grade estimate. Compression members are stressed about equally throughout, and no limitation related to location of knots is imposed. In tension, knots along the edge of a member cause an eccentricity that induces bending stresses, and they should therefore be more restricted than knots away from the edge. In simply supported structural members subjected to bending, stresses are greater in the middle of the length and at the top and bottom edges than at mid-height. These facts are recognized in some grades by different limitations on the sizes of knots in different locations.

Knot sizes are likely to be difficult to assess on many members in historic bridges. A scale is often used for quick estimates of knot size. Anthony et al. (2009) discuss another useful technique (a grid on a clear film) for estimating

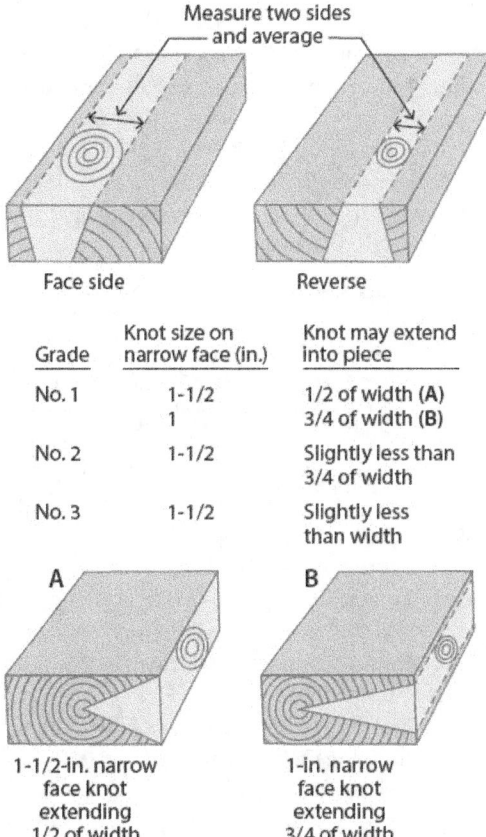

Figure 9.5—Adaptation of diagram from a pocket guide showing measurement of knots on 2-inch to 4-inch lumber which included structural joists and planks (Southern Pine Grading Rule 2002, used by permission, Southern Pine Inspection Bureau 2002).

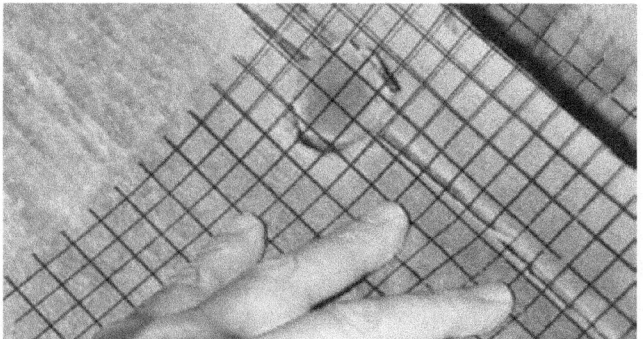

Figure 9.6—Example of using grid to establish the size of knot in bridge member. The measured knot in the example is 1-1/2 in.

knots in dimension lumber. When properly aligned, the grid allows you to make a good estimate of knot size to the closest 1/4 inch (Fig. 9.6). Accurately capturing maximum knot size for the centerline and edge of the member is highly important; these are usually the controlling features for establishing grade.

Slope of grain

Slope of grain is a ratio expressing the amount the grain slopes up or down within a set distance along the long axis of the member (Fig. 9.7). A nonzero slope of grain (cross grain) reduces mechanical properties of lumber. Severely cross-grained pieces are also undesirable because they tend to warp with changes in moisture content. Stresses caused by shrinkage during drying are greater in structural lumber than in small, clear, straight-grained specimens and are increased in zones of sloping or distorted grain. To provide a margin of safety, the reduction in design properties resulting from cross grain in visually graded structural lumber is considerably greater than that observed in small, clear specimens that contain similar cross grain.

Average line of the direction of fibers

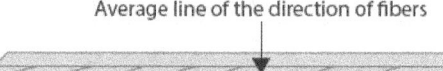
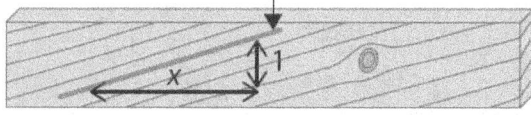

Figure 9.7—Definition of slope of grain is the ratio of rise to run (1:x).

Measuring slope of grain

Drying checks in timber generally follow the slope of grain and can be used to determine the slope of grain on painted timbers. Figure 9.8 shows an example of how checks indicate the slope of grain of a member. Other times the grain will be obvious on the unfinished surfaces of a member.

To measure slope of grain, the clear sheet with a printed 1/2-in. grid can once again be put to use (Fig. 9.9). In this example, the area that appears to have significant slope of grain should be measured from an axis parallel to the long axis of the member. The grid can be used to establish the rise-over-run ratio. To do so, the total number of inches for the rise can be determined along the vertical axis by counting from the lowest point of the rise to the highest point

Figure 9.8—Example of using checking in a member to measure the slope of grain in bridge. The end of the scale points to the start of one check.

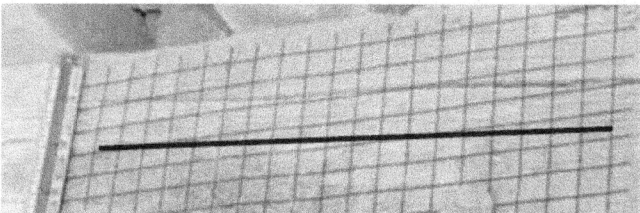

Figure 9.9—Use of grid to easily estimate the slope of grain. The 2:18 grids above implies 1 in 9 slope of grain. The black line shows the direction of slope of grain.

of the rise (or wherever the grain crosses the edge of the acetate sheet). The total number of inches in the run can be determined along the horizontal axis by counting across from the lowest point of the rise to the highest point of the rise (or wherever the grain crosses the edge of the acetate sheet). These measurements can then be used to represent the actual slope of grain over a given length to determine the appropriate grade. As with knots, the most severe slope of grain in a member should be identified and, depending on its severity, may be the limiting factor for grade.

Decay

Decay in most forms should be prohibited or severely restricted in stress grades because the extent of decay is difficult to determine and its effect on strength is often greater than visual observation would indicate (Gonzalez and Morrell 2012). Decay of the pocket type (for example, *Fomes pini*) can be permitted to some extent in stress grades, as can decay that occurs in knots but does not extend into the surrounding wood. But if evidence of extensive decay is present, replacing the member is the best option.

Measuring decay

In a field inspection, decay can be detected by a close examination of texture and color of the wood. Decay can be indicated by color and/or texture changes such as brown, cubical, friable wood, or by soft, white, brittle wood. Decay would also clearly be suggested by the presence of mushrooms or other fruiting bodies. Also, the absence of wood can be suggestive of decay. Decay is often more severe where moisture collects or is trapped, such as where two pieces of wood overlap, or where fasteners penetrate the wood. A probe can be used to determine if wood structure is weakened (Chapter 10).

Checks, splits, and shake
Checks and splits have little influence on Post and Timber members but can affect the behavior of Beam and Stringer members. Shake in a Beam and Stringer is measured between lines enclosing the shake and parallel to the wide face.

Checks and splits
Checks are separations on the surface of the wood that normally occur as a result of drying wood. Splits are a separation of the wood through the piece to the opposite surface or to an adjoining face. Checks and splits are rated by only the area of actual opening. An end-split is considered equal to an end-check that extends through the full thickness of the piece. The effects of checks and splits on strength and the principles of their limitation are the same as those for shake (below).

Shake
Shake (or "ring-shake") is the separation of annual rings caused by weak or absent bonds between them and is presumed to extend lengthwise within a member without limit. Because shake reduces resistance to shear in members subjected to bending, grading rules therefore restrict shake most closely in those parts of a bending member (Beam and Stringer) where shear stresses are highest. In members with limited cross-grain, which are subjected only to tension or compression (Post and Timber), shake does not affect strength greatly. Shake may also be limited in a grade because of appearance and because it permits entrance of moisture, which can result in decay.

Measuring checks, splits, and shake
How checks, splits, and shake are measured depends on the intended use of the member. For all grades of members

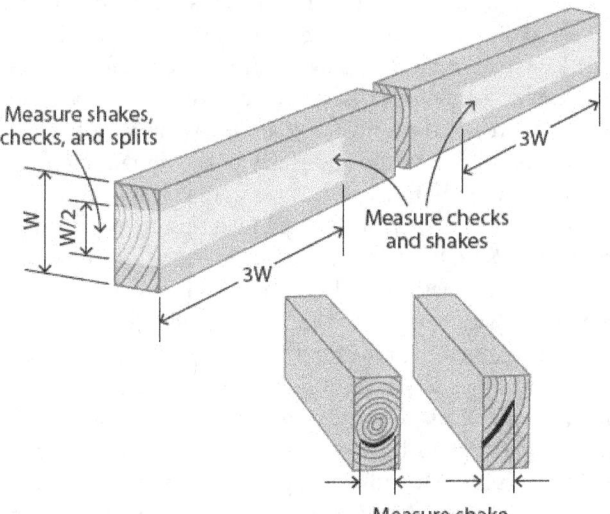

Figure 9.10—Beams and stringer checks, shake, and split measurement.

intended to be used as Beam and Stringer, checks, splits, and shake are measured in the middle half of the width. Restrictions on checks apply for a distance from the ends equal to three times the width of the wide face. Shake is measured from the end grain of the member between lines enclosing the shake and parallel to the wide face (Fig. 9.10). Checks are measured as an average of the penetration perpendicular to the wide face (Fig. 9.11). Where two or more checks appear on the same face, only the deepest one is measured. Where two checks are directly opposite each other, the sum of their deepest penetration is considered. Splits are measured as the penetration of a split from the end of the piece and parallel to the edges of the piece (Fig. 9.12).

In Post and Timber, shake is measured at the ends of pieces, between lines parallel with the two faces that give the least dimension (Fig. 9.13). If the member is below 16% moisture content, the size of the shake may be 1.5 times the size permitted in the grade.

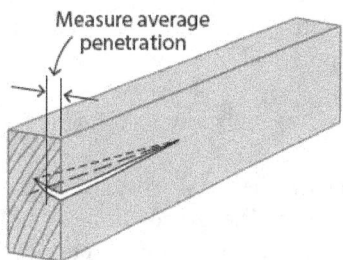

Figure 9.11—Checks in post and timber.

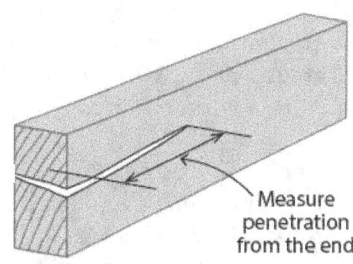

Figure 9.12—Split measurement.

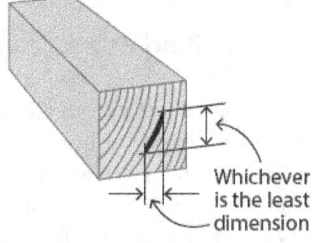

Figure 9.13—Shake in post and timber.

9.3.5 Density, rate of growth, and percentage of latewood
The strength and stiffness of clear wood are related to its density, with denser wood generally being stronger and stiffer than less dense wood. In some species, based on the structure of the wood, rate of growth (rings per inch) and percentage of latewood can give an indication of the density

of the wood. Strength is related to mass per unit volume (density) of clear wood. Properties assigned to lumber are sometimes modified by using rate of growth and percentage of latewood as measures of density. Typically, selection for density requires that rings per unit length and percentage of latewood be within a specified range. Some very low-strength pieces can be eliminated from a grade by excluding those that are exceptionally low in density.

9.3.6 Heartwood and sapwood
Heartwood or sapwood is often not taken into account in structural grading because heartwood and sapwood are assumed to have essentially equal mechanical properties. However, heartwood is sometimes specified in a visual grade because heartwood of some species is more resistant to decay than is sapwood. If heartwood of a particular species is decay resistant, heartwood may be specified for replacement members if the wood is to be untreated and will be exposed to a decay hazard. On the other hand, sapwood takes preservative treatment more readily than does heartwood and is preferable for lumber that will be treated with preservatives.

9.3.7 Pitch pockets
Pitch pockets ordinarily have so little effect on structural lumber that they can be disregarded in stress grading if they are small and limited in number. The presence of a large number of pitch pockets, however, may indicate shake or weakness of bond between annual rings, and extremely large pitch pockets may function as areas of ring shake and thus can be treated as such for grading purposes.

9.3.8 Wane
Wane refers to bark or lack of wood on the edge or corner of a piece of lumber. Requirements of appearance, fabrication, or ample bearing or nailing surfaces generally impose stricter limitations on wane than does strength. Wane is therefore limited in structural lumber on those bases rather than for its influence on timber strength.

9.4 What to prioritize in field estimation grading
When inspecting a bridge, not all properties discussed above will be easily measured. Fortunately, the most significant strength-reducing factors in structural members of wooden bridges (size and location of the largest knots, slope of grain, and presence of decay) are some of the most easily field-assessable characteristics. The most time and greatest care should be taken to measure these properties on the critical members. Next in importance would be determining rings per inch, if possible, to give an indication of relative density of the member. If these properties are available, an approximation of grade can be established and thereby a reasonable first estimate of design values for the member should be attainable.

9.5 Examples of grade estimation
Nine example members from different bridges are tabulated in Table 9.6 to illustrate estimation of grade for a member. Entries 1 to 6 look at dimension lumber members; entries 7 to 9 look at the grade of timber size members.

9.5.1 Dimension lumber grading examples
Six dimension lumber member grade estimation examples are presented in Table 9.6. Member 1 was identified as a piece of red oak and had a measured dimension of a full 3 by 8 in., making it a structural joist and plank. No grade stamp was present. There was, however, considerable decay present in this member. Even though the knot sizes and slope of grain for a 3 by 8 member, based on the criteria in Table 9.3, would have allowed for an estimated grade of No. 1, the presence of severe decay made this member a candidate for replacement.

Member 2 was identified as Douglas-fir, with measured dimensions of 1.5 by 5.5 in. It was in good shape with a clearly marked No. 1 grade stamp. Because there was no indication of decay or damage, the stamped grade will be used.

The initial inspection of member 3 indicated that the member was northern red oak and in good shape with no damage or decay present. Member 3 was a full 2 by 6 in. and can be considered a structural joist and plank. No grade stamp was present. There was good access to all sides of the member for over 70% of its length. Measured slope of grain and knot dimensions were compared with allowable knot sizes and slope of grain for a 2 by 6 shown in Table 9.3. Member 3 grades out as a Select Structural grade member according to its slope of grain, but the knot characteristics are that of a No. 2 member. The grade level that a member qualifies for always takes the lowest estimated grade characteristic for the member. Therefore, the grade for member 3 is estimated to be No. 2.

The initial inspection of member 4 identified the species as cottonwood and again indicated that the member was in good shape with no damage or decay present. Member 4 had measured dimensions that were closest to the dimensions of a piece of nominal 2 by 8 dimension lumber and could be considered a structural joist and plank. There was very good access to three of the four sides for 50% of this member, with limited access to the wide face for the remaining portions of the member. Lack of access to the faces of the member makes the estimate of grade of this member more uncertain. Using the criteria detailed in Table 9.3, the tabulated knot information available suggests the grade is No. 1, whereas the slope of grain value only qualifies for No. 2. Therefore estimated grade for member 4 is No. 2.

The initial inspection identified member 5 as Southern Pine with no decay present. Member 5 had a measured dimension of a full 2 by 4 in. and can be classified as a structural light framing member. No grade stamp was present. There was very good access to all sides of the member. The knot dimensions and slope of grain were compared against the criteria found in Table 9.3. One large edge knot on the wide face forced a reduction in the estimated grade for member 5 to No. 2.

The initial inspection identified member 6 as American chestnut. Member 6 had a measured cross-sectional dimension of 2 by 6 in. There was good access to all sides of the member for 80% of its length. A probe test revealed no severe decay, and no other damage was observed. Applying the criteria in the national grading rule in Table 9.3 for dimension lumber, the recorded knot sizes and slope of grain suggest an approximate grade of No. 2 for member 6.

9.5.2 Timber grading example

Three timber grading examples are presented in Table 9.6. The initial inspection identified member 7 as Southern Pine. Member 7 had measured dimensions of 5.5 by 7.5 in. The dimension of this member allows it to be treated as a nominal 6 by 8 Post and Timber. Because the member is Southern Pine and Southern Pine grading rules do not distinguish between Beam and Stringer or Post and Timber, only one criterion for knots and slope of grain is given in Table 9.4. Initial inspection of the member indicated that the member was in good shape with no damage present or obvious signs of decay. There was good access to all sides of the member for over 50% of its length and access to three sides for the remaining length of the member. The estimated slope of grain information for member 7 is No. 1.

The initial inspection identified member 8 as Douglas-fir and indicated that the member was in good shape with no damage present or obvious signs of decay. Member 8 had a measured dimension of 7.5 by 9.5 in.. This member was being used as a support column and had all sides visible. The dimension and use of this timber make it a Post or Timber. The Post and Timber rules presented in Table 9.5 can be applied to Douglas-fir timbers. There were very few and quite small knots present in this member. Member 8 easily met the criteria for Select Structural.

The initial inspection identified Member 9 as ash and indicated that the member was in good shape with no damage present or obvious signs of decay. Member 9 had a measured dimension of 5 by 8 in. The dimension and use of this member makes it a Beam and Stringer. The grading rules for timber Beam and Stringer are given in Table 9.5. There was good access to only three sides of the member for over 70% of its length. The member knot sizes indicated the beam could be graded out as a No. 1 but a severe slope of grain downgraded member 9 to No. 2.

9.6 Words of advice for size and grade estimation

This manual is meant to provide the reader with very basic information about how grading is conducted and a very basic method for estimating grade for members. The most accurate estimate of the in-place grade of a member would be obtained by certified graders that have extensive experience and knowledge of various structural lumber grades.

The field inspector, however, should be able to get a good idea of the species of the wood and the size and quality of the members that are in the structure.

Keep good records indicating the amount of each member that was accessible and your confidence of the estimated grade. Many times it will be impossible to see a large portion of a member, and you truly will need to make an educated guess that, based on what you can see, the same knots and slope of grain conditions may extend to the rest of the member. To arrive at an estimate of the design value for the member, the condition and your confidence in the estimate of grade is important.

Table 9.1—Strength properties of some commercially important woods grown in the United States (metric)[a]

Common species names	Moisture content	Specific gravity[b]	Static bending			Impact bending (mm)	Compression parallel to grain (kPa)	Compression perpendicular to grain (kPa)	Shear parallel to grain (kPa)	Tension perpendicular to grain (kPa)	Side hardness (N)
			Modulus of rupture (kPa)	Modulus of elasticity[c] (MPa)	Work to maximum load (kJ/m^3)						
Hardwoods											
Ash, White	Green	0.55	66,000	9,900	108	970	27,500	4,600	9,300	4,100	4,300
	12%	0.60	103,000	12,000	115	1,090	51,100	8,000	13,200	6,500	5,900
Aspen, Quaking	Green	0.35	35,000	5,900	44	560	14,800	1,200	4,600	1,600	1,300
	12%	0.38	58,000	8,100	52	530	29,300	2,600	5,900	1,800	1,600
Beech, American	Green	0.56	59,000	9,500	82	1,090	24,500	3,700	8,900	5,000	3,800
	12%	0.64	103,000	11,900	104	1,040	50,300	7,000	13,900	7,000	5,800
Birch, Yellow	Green	0.55	57,000	10,300	111	1,220	23,300	3,000	7,700	3,000	3,600
	12%	0.62	114,000	13,900	143	1,400	56,300	6,700	13,000	6,300	5,600
Chestnut, American	Green	0.40	39,000	6,400	48	610	17,000	2,100	5,500	3,000	1,900
	12%	0.43	59,000	8,500	45	480	36,700	4,300	7,400	3,200	2,400
Elm, American	Green	0.46	50,000	7,700	81	970	20,100	2,500	6,900	4,100	2,800
	12%	0.50	81,000	9,200	90	990	38,100	4,800	10,400	4,600	3,700
Elm, Rock	Green	0.57	66,000	8,200	137	1,370	26,100	4,200	8,800	—	—
	12%	0.63	102,000	10,600	132	1,420	48,600	8,500	13,200	—	—
Hickory, Shagbark	Green	0.64	76,000	10,800	163	1,880	31,600	5,800	10,500	—	6,500
	12%	0.72	139,000	14,900	178	1,700	63,500	12,100	16,800	—	8,400
Maple, Red	Green	0.49	53,000	9,600	79	810	2,260	2,800	7,900	—	3,100
	12%	0.54	92,000	11,300	86	810	45,100	6,900	12,800	—	4,200
Maple, Sugar	Green	0.56	65,000	10,700	92	1020	27,700	4,400	10,100	—	4,300
	12%	0.63	109,000	12,600	114	990	54,000	10,100	16,100	—	6,400
Oak, Northern Red	Green	0.56	57,000	9,300	91	1,120	23,700	4,200	8,300	5,200	4,400
	12%	0.63	99,000	12,500	100	1,090	46,600	7,000	12,300	5,500	5,700
Oak, Southern Red	Green	0.52	48,000	7,900	55	740	20,900	3,800	6,400	3,300	3,800
	12%	0.59	75,000	10,300	65	660	42,000	6,000	9,600	3,500	4,700
Oak, White	Green	0.60	57,000	8,600	80	1,070	24,500	4,600	8,600	5,300	4,700
	12%	0.68	105,000	12,300	102	940	51,300	7,400	13,800	5,500	6,000
Sycamore, American	Green	0.46	45,000	7,300	52	660	20,100	2,500	6,900	4,300	2,700
	12%	0.49	69,000	9,800	59	660	37,100	4,800	10,100	5,000	3,400
Yellow-poplar	Green	0.40	41,000	8,400	52	660	18,300	1,900	5,400	3,500	2,000
	12%	0.42	70,000	10,900	61	610	38,200	3,400	8,200	3,700	2,400

Table 9.1—Strength properties of some commercially important woods grown in the United States (metric)[a]—con.

| Common species names | Moisture content | Specific gravity[b] | Static bending | | | Impact bending (mm) | Compression parallel to grain (kPa) | Compression perpendicular to grain (kPa) | Shear parallel to grain (kPa) | Tension perpendicular to grain (kPa) | Side hardness (N) |
			Modulus of rupture (kPa)	Modulus of elasticity[c] (MPa)	Work to maximum load (kJ/m³)						
Softwoods											
Baldcypress	Green	0.42	46,000	8,100	46	640	24,700	2,800	6,500	2,100	1,700
	12%	0.46	73,000	9,900	57	610	43,900	5,000	6,900	1,900	2,300
Cedar, Western	Green	0.31	35,900	6,500	34	430	19,100	1,700	5,300	1,600	1,200
	12%	0.32	51,700	7,700	40	430	31,400	3,200	6,800	1,500	1,600
Douglas-fir, Coast	Green	0.45	53,000	10,800	52	660	26,100	2,600	6,200	2,100	2,200
	12%	0.48	85,000	13,400	68	790	49,900	5,500	7,800	2,300	3,200
Fir, Balsam	Green	0.33	38,000	8,600	32	410	18,100	1,300	4,600	1,200	1,300
	12%	0.35	63,000	10,000	35	510	36,400	2,800	6,500	1,200	1,700
Fir, Noble	Green	0.37	43,000	9,500	41	480	20,800	1,900	5,500	1,600	1,300
	12%	0.39	74,000	11,900	61	580	42,100	3,600	7,200	1,500	1,800
Hemlock, Eastern	Green	0.38	44,000	7,400	46	530	21,200	2,500	5,900	1,600	1,800
	12%	0.40	61,000	8,300	47	530	37,300	4,500	7,300	—	2,200
Hemlock, Western	Green	0.42	46,000	9,000	48	560	23,200	1,900	5,900	2,000	1,800
	12%	0.45	78,000	11,300	57	580	49,000	3,800	8,600	2,300	2,400
Larch, Western	Green	0.48	53,000	10,100	71	740	25,900	2,800	6,000	2,300	2,300
	12%	0.52	90,000	12,900	87	890	52,500	6,400	9,400	3,000	3,700
Pine, Eastern White	Green	0.34	34,000	6,800	36	430	16,800	1,500	4,700	1,700	1,300
	12%	0.35	59,000	8,500	47	460	33,100	3,000	6,200	2,100	1,700
Pine, Jack	Green	0.40	41,000	7,400	50	660	20,300	2,100	5,200	2,500	1,800
	12%	0.43	68,000	9,300	57	690	39,000	4,000	8,100	2,900	2,500
Pine, Loblolly	Green	0.47	50,000	9,700	57	760	24,200	2,700	5,900	1,800	2,000
	12%	0.51	88,000	12,300	72	760	49,200	5,400	9,600	3,200	3,100
Pine, Lodgepole	Green	0.38	38,000	7,400	39	510	18,000	1,700	4,700	1,500	1,500
	12%	0.41	65,000	9,200	47	510	37,000	4,200	6,100	2,000	2,100
Pine, Longleaf	Green	0.54	59,000	11,000	61	890	29,800	3,300	7,200	2,300	2,600
	12%	0.59	100,000	13,700	81	860	58,400	6,600	10,400	3,200	3,900
Pine, Ponderosa	Green	0.38	35,000	6,900	36	530	16,900	1,900	4,800	2,100	1,400
	12%	0.40	65,000	8,900	49	480	36,700	4,000	7,800	2,900	2,000
Pine, Red	Green	0.41	40,000	8,800	42	660	18,800	1,800	4,800	2,100	1,500
	12%	0.46	76,000	11,200	68	660	41,900	4,100	4,800	3,200	2,500
Spruce, Red	Green	0.37	41,000	9,200	48	460	18,800	1,800	5,200	1,500	1,600
	12%	0.40	74,000	11,400	58	640	38,200	3,800	8,900	2,400	2,200
Spruce, Sitka	Green	0.37	39,000	5,800	43	610	18,400	1,900	5,200	1,700	1,600
	12%	0.40	70,000	10,800	65	640	38,700	4,000	7,900	2,600	2,300

[a]Results of tests on clear specimens in the green and air-dried conditions. These values are average measured properties of small clear specimens in a laboratory setting and are not design values. Definition of properties: impact bending is height of drop that causes complete failure, using 0.71-kg (50-lb) hammer; compression parallel to grain is also called maximum crushing strength; compression perpendicular to grain is fiber stress at proportional limit; shear is maximum shearing strength; tension is maximum tensile stregth; and side hardness is hardness measured when load is perpendicular to grain.

[b]Specific gravity is based on weight when ovendry and volume when green or at 12% moisture content.

[c]Modulus of elasticity measured from a simply supported, center-loaded beam, on a span depth ratio of 14/1. To correct for shear deflection, the modulus can be increased by 10%.

Table 9.2—Specifications for dimension of structural members (DOC PS 20)

Thicknesses					Widths				
	Minimum dressed					Minimum dressed			
	Dry		Green			Dry		Green	
Nominal in.	mm	in.	mm	in.	Nominal in.	mm	in.	mm	in.
Board									
					2	38	1-1/2	40	1-9/16
					3	64	2-1/2	65	2-9/16
					4	89	3-1/2	90	3-9/16
3/8	8	5/16	9	11/32	5	114	4-1/2	117	4-5/8
1/2	11	7/16	12	15/32	6	140	5-1/2	143	5-5/8
5/8	14	9/16	15	19/32	7	165	6-1/2	168	6-5/8
3/4	16	5/8	17	11/16	8	184	7-1/4	190	7-1/2
1	19	3/4	20	25/32	9	210	8-1/4	216	8-1/2
1-1/4	25	1	26	1-1/32	10	235	9-1/4	241	9-1/2
1-1/2	32	1-1/4	33	1-9/32	11	260	10-1/4	267	10-1/2
					12	286	11-1/4	292	11-1/2
					14	337	13-1/4	343	13-1/2
					16	387	15-1/4	394	15-1/2
Dimension									
					2	38	1-1/2	40	1-9/16
					2-1/2	51	2	52	2-1/16
					3	64	2-1/2	65	2-9/16
2	38	1-1/2	40	1-9/16	3-1/2	76	3	78	3-1/16
2-1/2	51	2	52	2-1/16	4	89	3-1/2	90	3-9/16
3	64	2-1/2	65	2-9/16	4-1/2	102	4	103	4-1/16
3-1/2	76	3	78	3-1/16	5	114	4-1/2	117	4-5/8
4	89	3-1/2	90	3-9/16	6	140	5-1/2	143	5-5/8
4-1/2	102	4	103	4-1/16	8	184	7-1/4	190	7-1/2
					10	235	9-1/4	241	9-1/2
					12	286	11-1/4	292	11-1/2
					14	337	13-1/4	343	13-1/2
					16	387	15-1/4	394	15-1/2
Timbers									
5 & 6 thick	13 off	1/2 off	13 off	1/2 off	5 & 6 wide	13 off	1/2 off	13 off	1/2 off
7–15 thick	19 off	3/4 off	13 off	1/2 off	7–15 wide	19 off	3/4 off	13 off	1/2 off
≥ 16 thick	25 off	1 off	13 off	1/2 off	≥ 16 wide	25 off	1 off	13 off	1/2 off

Table 9.3—National Grading Rule Specifications for Dimension Lumber (Standard Grading Rules for Southern Pine Lumber 2002; used courtesy of Southern Pine Inspection Bureau)

Characteristics	Select Structural			No. 1			No. 2			No. 3		
Compression wood	← Not allowed in damaging form for the grade considered →											
Slope of grain	1 in 12			1 in 10			1 in 8			1 in 4		
Decay	Not permitted			Not permitted			Heart center, 1/3 thickness × 1/3 width			Heart center, 1/3 cross section. Must not destroy nailing edge. See para. 710(e).		
Holes	Same as unsound knots			Same as unsound knots			See chart below			See chart below		
Knots	Edge (in.)	Center-line (in.)	Unsound knots (in.)	Edge (in.)	Center-line (in.)	Unsound knots (in.)	Edge (in.)	Center-line (in.)	Holes (in.)	Edge (in.)	Center-line (in.)	Holes (in.)
2×4	3/4	7/8	3/4	1	1-1/2	1	1-1/4	2	1-1/4	1-3/4	2-1/2	1-3/4
2×5	1	1-1/2	7/8	1-1/4	1-7/8	1-1/8	1-5/8	2-3/8	1-3/8	2-1/4	3	1-7/8
2×6	1-1/8	1-7/8	1	1-1/2	2-1/4	1-1/4	1-7/8	2-7/8	1-1/2	2-3/4	3-3/4	2
2×8	1-1/2	2-1/4	1-1/4	2	2-3/4	1-1/2	2-1/2	3-1/2	2	3-1/2	4-1/2	2-1/2
2×10	1-7/8	2-5/8	1-1/4	2-1/2	3-1/4	1-1/2	3-1/4	4-1/4	2-1/2	4-1/2	5-1/2	3
2×12	2-1/4	3	1-1/4	3	3-3/4	1-1/2	3-3/4	4-3/4	3	5-1/2	6-1/2	3-1/2
	Sound, firm, encased, pith, tight and well spaced. One hole or equivalent smaller holes per 4 lin. ft.			Sound, firm, encased, pith, tight and well spaced. One hole or equivalent smaller holes per 3 lin. ft.			Well spaced knots of any quality. One hole or equivalent smaller holes per 2 lin. ft.			Well spaced knots of any quality. One hole or equivalent smaller holes per 1 lin. ft.		
Shakes	← Ends: Same as splits. Elsewhere: 2 ft surface; none through. →						Ends: Same as splits. Elsewhere: Surface 3 ft or 1/4 length; 2 ft through.			1/6 length if through at edges or ends; elsewhere through shakes 1/3 length.		
Checks	← Surface seasoning checks not limited. Through checks at ends limited as splits. →											
Skips	← Hit and miss in 10% of the pieces. See para. 720(f). →						Hit and miss. 5% of pieces may be hit or miss or heavy skip for 2 ft. See para. 720(e,f,g).			Hit or miss. 10% of pieces may have heavy skip. See para. 720(e,g).		
Splits	← Equal to the width →						Equal to 1-1/2 times the width			Equal to 1/6 length		
Wane	← 1/4 thickness × 1/4 width × full length or equivalent; must not exceed 1/2 thickness × 1/3 width for up to 1/4 length. Also see para. 750. →						1/3 thickness × 1/3 width × full length or equivalent; must not exceed 2/3 thickness × 1/2 width for up to 1/4 length. Also see para. 750.			1/2 thickness × 1/2 width × full length or equivalent; must not exceed 7/8 thickness or 3/4 width for up to 1/4 length. Also see para. 750.		
Bow	← 10 ft/1-3/8 in.; 12 ft/1-1/2 in.; 14 ft/2 in.; 16 ft/2-1/2 in. →						10 ft/1-1/2 in.; 12 ft/2 in.; 14 ft/2-1/2 in.; 16 ft/3-1/4 in.			10 ft/2-3/4 in.; 12 ft/3 in.; 14 ft/4 in.; 16 ft/5 in.		
Crook		10 ft	12 ft	14 ft	16 ft		10 ft	12 ft	14 ft	16 ft	10 ft	12 ft	14 ft	16 ft
2×4		3/8 in.	1/2 in.	5/8 in.	3/4 in.		1/2 in.	11/16 in.	7/8 in.	1 in.	3/4 in.	1 in.	1-1/4 in.	1-1/2 in.
2×6	←	5/16 in.	7/16 in.	9/16 in.	11/16 in.	→	7/16 in.	5/8 in.	3/4 in.	7/8 in.	5/8 in.	7/8 in.	1-1/8 in.	1-3/8 in.
2×8		1/4 in.	13/32 in.	1/2 in.	9/16 in.		3/8 in.	1/2 in.	5/8 in.	3/4 in.	1/2 in.	13/16 in.	1 in.	1-1/8 in.
2×10		7/32 in.	3/8 in.	7/16 in.	1/2 in.		1/4 in.	7/16 in.	1/2 in.	5/8 in.	7/16 in.	3/4 in.	7/8 in.	1 in.
2×12		3/16 in.	9/32 in.	3/8 in.	7/16 in.		3/16 in.	3/8 in.	3/8 in.	1/2 in.	3/8 in.	9/16 in.	3/4 in.	7/8 in.

Dense grain: Requires 6 rings/in. and 1/3 summerwood or 4 rings/in. and 1/2 summerwood.

Exceptionally light weight pieces: Should not be placed in No. 2 and higher grades (exceptionally light weight pieces have less than 15% summerwood).

Table 9.4—Grading Rule Specifications for Southern Pine Timber (Standard Grading Rules for Southern Pine Lumber 2002; used courtesy of Southern Pine Inspection Bureau)

Grading rules for timbers								
Characteristics	**Select Structural**			**No. 1**			**No. 2**	
Compression wood	Not allowed in damaging form for the grade considered							
Slope of grain	1 in 14			1 in 11			1 in 6	
Decay	In knots only			In knots only			Heart-center decay or unsound red heart and equiv. streaks limited to 10% cross section if wholly enclosed within four surfaces of each piece and 5% otherwise	
Holes	Medium – well scattered			Medium – well scattered			Limited to 1-1/2 in. in diameter	
Knots (nominal width of face) (in.)	Narrow face and at edge of wide face (in.) (2)	Centerline wide face (in.)	Unsound knots (in.) (1)	Narrow face and at edge of wide face (in.) (2)	Centerline wide face (in.)	Unsound knots (in.) (1)	Narrow face and at edge of wide face; centerline wide face (in.)	Unsound knots (in.) (1)
5	1-3/8		1	1-3/4		1-3/8	2-1/2	2
6	1-5/8	1-5/8	1-1/4	2-1/8	2-1/8	1-5/8	3	2-1/4
8	1-7/8	2-1/4	1-1/2	2-1/2	2-3/4	2	4-1/2	2-3/4
10	2-1/8	2-3/4	2	2-3/4	3-1/2	2-1/2	5-1/2	3
12	2-3/8	3-1/4	2-1/8	3-1/8	4-1/4	2-7/8	6-1/2	3-1/2
14	2-1/2	3-5/8	2-1/4	3-3/8	4-3/4	3-1/8	7-1/2	3-3/4
16	2-3/4	3-7/8	2-1/2	3-1/2	5	3-3/8	8	4
18	2-7/8	4-1/8	2-1/2	3-1/2	5-1/4	3-1/2	8-1/2	4
20	3	4-3/8	3	3-1/2	5-1/2	3-1/2	9	4
	Sound, firm, encased, and pith knots			Sound, firm, encased, and pith knots			Sound, firm, encased, and pith knots	
	(1) In unsound knots as allowed, decay must be confined to the knot itself and not be in surrounding wood and not penetrate deeper than 1-1/2 in. (2) In timbers of equal face, knots are permitted throughout as specified for narrow faces regardless of location.						(1) In unsound knots as allowed, decay must not penetrate deeper than 2 in.	
Shakes, checks, splits	Splits not longer than thickness of piece; shakes and surface checks not deeper than 1/3 thickness if not dry and 3/8 thickness if dry			Splits not longer than thickness of piece; shakes and surface checks not deeper than 1/3 thickness if not dry and 3/8 thickness if dry			Splits not longer than 1-1/4 times thickness of piece; shakes and surface checks not deeper than 1/2 thickness	
Skips	Hit and Miss in 10% of pieces			Hit or Miss dressing			Hit or Miss dressing except occasional scant width and thickness from full length skip limited to 1/8 in., must be No. 1 otherwise throughout any portion scant over 1/16 in.	
Stain	Medium if dry; not limited if ordered green			Medium if dry; not limited if ordered green			Medium if dry; not limited if ordered green	
Wane	1/8 the width of face and 1/4 length			1/6 the width of face and 1/3 length			1/4 face on one edge and 1/3 face on both edges	
Warp	Very light			Very light			Light	

Table 9.5—Grading Rules Specifications for NeLMA (WWPA) Timbers

Beams and stringers								
Characteristics	**Select Structural**			**No. 1**			**No. 2**	
Slope of grain	1 in 14			1 in 10			1 in 6	
Decay	None			None			Small spots of unsound wood well scattered, 1/6 the face width	
Knots (nominal width of face) (in.)	Edge wide face (in.)	Centerline wide face (in.)	Unsound knots	Edge wide face (in.)	Centerline wide face (in.)	Unsound knots	Edge of wide face and centerline of wide face (in.)	Unsound knots
8	1-7/8	2		2-5/8	3		4-1/2	
10	2	2-5/8		2-7/8	3-3/4		5-5/8	
12	2-1/8	3-1/8		3-1/4	4-1/2		6-7/8	
14	2-3/8	3-3/8		3-1/2	5		7-1/2	
16	2-1/2	3-5/8		3-3/4	5-1/4		8-1/8	
18	2-3/4	3-5/8		3-7/8	5-5/8		8-5/8	
20	2-7/8	3-7/8		4-1/8	5-7/8		9-1/8	
22	3	4		4-3/8	6-1/4		9-1/2	
24	3-1/8	4-1/4		4-1/2	6-1/2		10	
	Sound, tight and well-spaced			Sound, tight and well-spaced			Sound, not firmly fixed or holes, well-spaced	
Shakes	1/6 the thickness on end			1/6 the thickness on end			1/2 length, 1/2 thickness. If through at ends, limited as splits.	
Splits	Splits equal in length to 1/2 the width of the piece or equivalent of end checks			Splits equal in length to width of the piece or equivalent of end checks			Medium or equivalent end checks	
Checks	Seasoning checks, single or opposite each other with a sum total equal to 1/4 the thickness of the piece			Seasoning checks, single or opposite each other with a sum total equal to 1/2 the thickness of the piece			Seasoning checks	
Skips	Occasional skips 1/16 in. deep, 2 ft in length			Occasional skips 1/8 in. deep, 2 ft in length			1/8 in. deep, 2 ft in length, or 1/16 in. skip full length	
Stain	Stained sapwood. Firm heart stain, 10% of width or equivalent.			Stained sapwood. Firm stained heartwood.			Stained wood	
Wane	1/8 of any face, or equivalent slightly more for a short distance			1/4 of any face or equivalent slightly more for a short distance			1/3 of any face, or equivalent slightly more for a short distance	

Table 9.5—Grading Rules Specifications for NeLMA (WWPA) Timbers—con.

Characteristics	Posts and timbers					
	Select Structural		**No. 1**		**No. 2**	
Slope of grain	1 in 12		1 in 10		1 in 6	
Decay	None		None		Small spots of unsound wood well scattered, 1/6 the face width	
Knots (nominal width of face) (in.)	Anywhere on wide face (in.)	Unsound knots (in.)	Anywhere on wide face (in.)	Unsound knots (in.)	Anywhere on wide face (in.)	Unsound knots (in.)
5	1		1-1/2		2-1/2	1-1/4
6	1-1/4		1-7/8		3	1-1/2
8	1-5/8		2-1/2		3-3/4	1-7/8
10	2		3-1/8		5	2-1/2
12	2-3/8		3-3/4		6	3
14	2-1/2		4		6-1/2	3-1/4
16	2-3/4		4-1/4		7	3-1/2
18	3		4-1/2		7-1/2	3-3/4
	Sound, tight and well-spaced		Sound, tight and well-spaced		Sound, not firmly fixed or holes, well-spaced	
Shakes	1/3 the thickness on end		1/3 the thickness on end		1/2 length, 1/2 thickness. If through at ends, limited as splits.	
Splits	Splits equal in length to 3/4 the thickness of the piece or equivalent of end checks		Splits equal in length to width of the piece or equivalent of end checks		Medium or equivalent end checks	
Checks	Seasoning checks, single or opposite each other with a sum total equal to 1/2 the thickness of the piece		Seasoning checks, single or opposite each other with a sum total equal to 1/2 the thickness of the piece		Seasoning checks	
Skips	Occasional skips 1/16 in. deep, 2 ft in length		Occasional skips 1/8 in. deep, 2 ft in length		1/8 in. deep, 2 ft in length, or 1/16 in. skip full length	
Stain	Stained sapwood. Firm heart stain, 10% of width or equivalent.		Stained sapwood. Firm stained heartwood.		Stained wood	
Wane	1/8 of any face, or equivalent slightly more for a short distance		1/4 of any face, or equivalent slightly more for a short distance		1/3 of any face, or equivalent slightly more for a short distance	

Table 9.6—Examples for estimation of member grade (members are not all from same bridge)

Member and species	Member size (in.)	Use	Percent access to the member and sides	Damage or decay present	Grade Stamp	Largest unsound knot (in.)	Largest edge knot on wide face (in.)	Largest center-line knot on wide face (in.)	Largest narrow face knot (in.)	Slope of grain (1:x)	Final estimated grade
1 Red Oak	3 by 8	Str. J&P	60% 3 of 4	Yes	No	N/A	N/A	N/A	N/A	N/A	
Grade estimate											Replace
2 Douglas-fir	1.5 by 5.5	Str. J&P	70% all	No	Yes	N/A	N/A	N/A	N/A	N/A	
Grade estimate					No. 1						No. 1
3 Northern Red Oak	2 by 6	Str. J&P	70% all	No	No	1.5	1.75	2.75	1.5	1:12	
Grade estimate						No. 2	No. 2	No. 2	N/A	Sel. Str.	No. 2
4 Cotton-wood	2 by 7.5	Str. J&P	50% 3 of 4	No	No	1.25	2.0	2.75	2.0	1:9	
Grade estimate						Sel. Str.	No. 1	No. 1	N/A	No. 2	No. 2
5 Southern Pine	2 by 4	Str. LF	100% all	No	No	0.75	1.25	1.25	0.5	1:18	
Grade estimate						Sel. Str.	No. 2	No. 1	N/A	Sel. Str.	No. 2
6 American Chestnut	2 by 6	Str. J&P	80% all	No	No	1.5	2.0	2.5	2.75	1:8	
Grade estimate						No. 2	No. 1	No. 2	N/A	No. 2	No. 2
7 Southern Pine	5.5 by 7.5	P-T	50% all 3 of 4 rest	No	No	1.5	2.25	2.75	2.0	1:12	
Grade estimate						Sel. Str.	No. 1	No. 1	No. 1	No. 1	No. 1
8 Douglas-fir	7.5 by 9.5	P-T	100% all	No	No	1	1	1.25	1	1:18	
Grade estimate						Sel. Str.	Sel. Str.	Sel. Str.	Sel. Str.	Sel. Str.	Sel. Str.
9 White Ash	5 by 8	B-S	70% 3 of 4	No	No	1.5	3.0	3.5	2.75	1:6	
Grade estimate						No. 1	No. 1	No. 1	No. 1	No. 2	No. 2

Str. J&P: Structural Joist and Plank (2–4 in. thick, 5 in. and wider).

Str. LF: Structural Light Framing (2–4 in. thick, 2–4 in. wide).

P-T: Post or Timber (5 by 5 in. and larger, width not more than 2 in. greater than thickness).

B-S: Beam or Stringer (5 in. and thicker, width more than 2 in. greater than thickness).

10 | Condition assessment of bridge members

The principal reason for most inspections of a wooden bridge is to determine the condition of the wood components so that a judgment can be made on the capacity of the bridge. Helpful tips and methods for conducting condition assessments of wood structures have been described in detail by many authors (Wood 1954; Ross et al. 2004; Brashaw et al. 2005a,b; Anthony 2007; Anthony et al. 2009; Anthony & Associates 2009; Kukay et al. 2013). These publications emphasize where problems are most likely to occur in historic wooden structures. Missing or failed components, wood in ground contact, wood with moisture stains, wood with the presence of fungal fruiting bodies, decayed wood at material interfaces, wood with insect bore holes and mud tubes, sill beams and plates in contact with masonry, burned or charred wood, and corroded or damaged fasteners or connections are all areas that are referred to as needing close inspection. If extensive decay or evidence of large-scale insect attack are present, the member is most likely compromised and should be replaced. Decay and insect attack can result in severe reduction in strength of the members (Gonzalez and Morrell 2012). Also, structurally damaged members (members that have already failed) need to be replaced. Choices of members to inspect depend on the goal of the inspection.

10.1 Sampling for condition assessment from covered bridges

For bridges, inspections should focus on areas where problems are known to be common, such as places where wood is in ground contact, moisture stains are present, or visible signs of decay are indicated. Areas where different types of material come in contact (such as wood and masonry) are other priority locations for condition assessment. These are areas such as beam pockets, floor joists and girders, roof framing, sill beams and plates (particularly when in contact with masonry), and top plates. Of less structural importance are the exterior wood work components, including cladding, shingles, and soffits. Flaws in the exterior wood cladding of a bridge, though, can be the point where moisture enters and damages structural elements. Finally, areas of the bridge that may have been modified should be closely examined to see if the modifications weakened the bridge.

10.2 Moisture-related degradation

An inspector should also be alert to areas where periodic leaks in roofs or walls or seasonal flooding may have caused serious problems with decay or warping. This is best accomplished by looking for evidence of moisture stains. It is important to differentiate moisture stains that resulted from a single exposure to moisture (Fig. 10.1) and those that represent a repeated exposure to moisture. Different hues of stain colors are an indication of repeated moisture exposure. One-time moisture exposures likely have little

Figure 10.1—Indication of a water exposure event. Note the single color of stained material. If this were from multiple wetting events, multiple colors or bands of stains would be evident.

Figure 10.2—Example of insect damage.

Figure 10.3—Failed load bearing member in need of replacement.

impact on the structural integrity of wood as long as there is sufficient air circulation to dry the member out. Repeated exposure to moisture, however, leads to decay and insect attack (Fig. 10.2). Determining member moisture content with moisture meters, described in Section 10.4.2, is a good way to determine if the moisture exposure has persisted to the time of inspection.

10.3 Physical degradation

An inspector should look for signs of damaged or missing members (Fig. 10.3). Physical degradation can either be a result of prolonged changes in climate (causing weathering or drying checks from shrinkage of large members as they

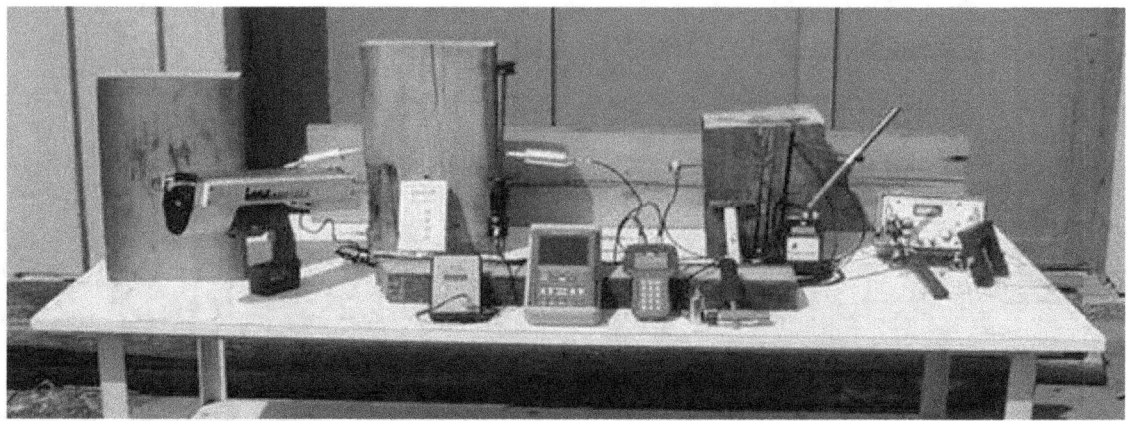

Figure 10.4—Various tools and techniques available to conduct condition assessments (used with permission of Natural Resources Research Institute, University of Minnesota Duluth, Brashaw et al. 2005b).

dry) or be a result of use (such as overloading or mechanical damage by careless drivers). Members that have clear evidence of physical damage should be replaced.

10.4 Nondestructive evaluation techniques

Nondestructive evaluation tests on various bridge members can help an inspector identify degradation of members caused by decay or physical damage. Many available methods are available for nondestructive evaluation (Fig. 10.4). The most widely applied techniques are described in greater detail in publications by Ross et al. (2004) and Brashaw et al. (2005a,b). A summary of the more common techniques follows.

10.4.1 Visual inspection

A quick walk around the bridge gives an inspector invaluable information and will suggest a starting point for more in-depth assessment. Look for any indication of decay or damage of structural members. Identify failed abutments (missing pieces, cracks in surface of abutment, sloping bridge deck, or other evidence of settling) or signs of overall deterioration of the bridge (failed members, excessive deflections, large gaps, missing members). Examine the surfaces of existing members looking for fungal fruiting bodies, sunken or collapsed faces or localized surface depressions, staining or discoloration, plant or moss growth in splits, cracks, insect damage, or fire damage. If present, these features are areas that will require the closest inspection.

10.4.2 Moisture meter

As previously discussed, elevated moisture content is an indicator of a board likely to have decay. To determine if excess moisture is present, a moisture content measurement can be performed with an electrical-resistance-type moisture meter and 76-mm- (3-in.-) long insulated probe pins (Fig. 10.5) or surface moisture meters in accordance with ASTM D 4444 (ASTM 2013) requirements. Several types of moisture content measuring devices are available. Most require some correction for temperature and species (Pfaff and Garrahan 1984). Conditions are right for decay if

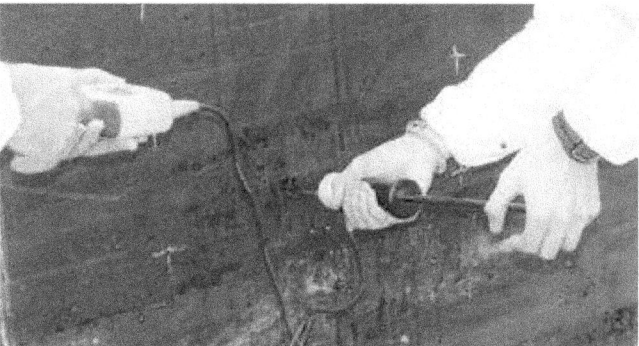

Figure 10.5—Example of a moisture meter in use.

moisture content is above 20%. Moisture content of sound wood should be between 6% and 12% for interior applications and between 10% and 20% for exterior applications. Decaying wood will often have moisture contents that register between 20% and 30% or higher. Previously decayed wood can be found in wet or dry members.

10.4.3 Probing

Another useful tool when looking for decay is an awl or knife to probe areas of suspected decay or insect damage. The probe should be used to see how solid the woody material is and how it fails when broken. A splintered break when you pry up a wood flake reveals sound wood while a brittle, brash (even, smooth transverse surface) break indicates decayed wood (Fig. 10.6). Care should be taken so that water-softened wood is not mistaken for decayed wood.

10.4.4 Increment boring

A forestry increment borer is not truly a nondestructive tool for inspecting (using an increment borer will leave a noticeable mark), but it is truly a useful tool for an inspector (Fig. 10.7). An increment borer can assist in identification of voids, indicate the presence or absence of decay, reveal the presence and penetration of treatment, and provide a potential sample for species identification. The hole created by boring should be plugged with a preservative-treated dowel to prevent a pathway for unwanted moisture exposure.

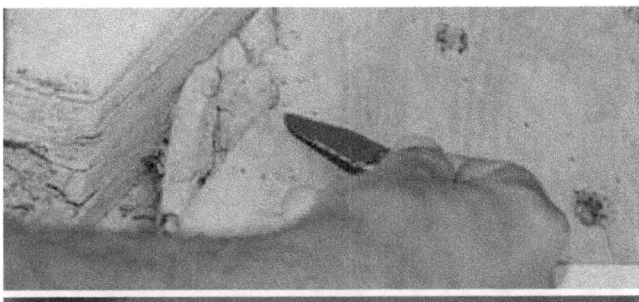

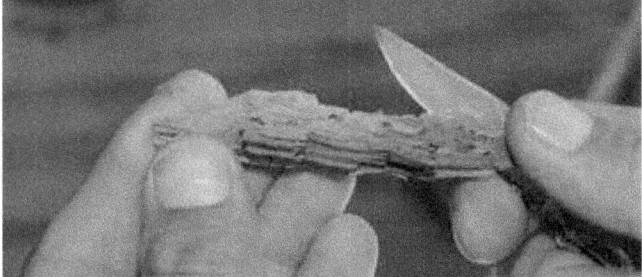

Figure 10.6—Example of a knife being used to probe wood: (top) Checking the soundness of wood and (bottom) an example of abrupt failure surfaces indicating decay.

Figure 10.7—Increment borer.

10.4.5 Stress wave

The calculated stress wave velocities (meters or feet per microsecond) of a bridge member can help identify potentially decayed locations in the member. Measurements of time-of-flight of induced stress waves within a member can be performed with stress wave timing equipment using well-established procedures (Fig. 10.8) (Ross et al. 1999). At locations of interest, the width of the member is measured along with the wave transmission time. A pulse is introduced into the member, and an accelerometer monitors the wave's arrival and stops the timing clock. Stress waves travel faster through sound wood than through unsound wood. Differences in transit time are used to indicate the location of decay. This method requires access to both sides of the member.

10.4.6 Resistance drilling

Another method of detecting decayed locations in bridge members is micro-resistance drilling. A micro-resistance drill measures drill bit resistance, and monitoring this resistance is a means of detecting unsound wood. There is far

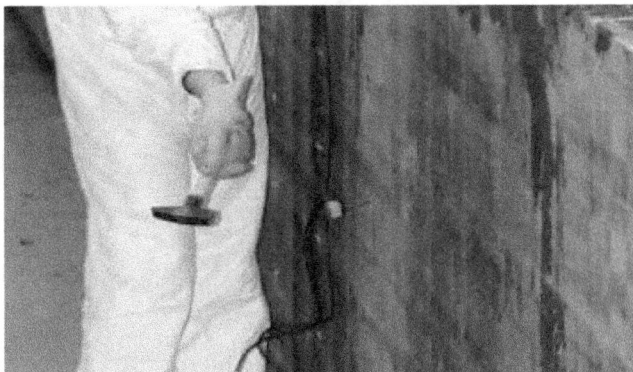

Figure 10.8—Transverse stress wave velocity measurement method.

Figure 10.9—Examples of nondestructive instruments in use.

less resistance to the drill in unsound wood. The drill measurement also provides a good density profile of the wood member. This method is further described by Ross et al. (2004) and Rinn (2013) (Fig. 10.9).

10.5 Importance of condition assessment

A member that is in poor condition, regardless of grade, can compromise the safety and integrity of a bridge. The inspector's confidence in the condition of members directly affects the design value estimate that can be assigned to that member. The more tools brought to bear on judging the condition of a member, the more confident an inspector can be in judging the condition of a member. This chapter gives only a few possible ways for an inspector to judge the condition of a member. Whole books are devoted to the topic. Any of the referenced articles, reports, or books are good resources for inspectors to improve their condition assessment skills.

10.6 Site-specific bridge condition assessment

In addition to the condition of individual members, some aspects of overall bridge condition should be evaluated (such as loss of bridge camber, changes in loading with changes in use) in a site-specific way that cannot be generalized for a field manual.

11 | Design value estimation

Wanting to assign structural lumber values to lumber found in historic structures is certainly nothing new. A 1954 article by Lyman Wood in *Southern Lumberman* explored issues associated with assigning structural design values to old lumber (Wood 1954). Loferski and others used nondestructive evaluation and testing techniques to determine mechanical properties (Loferski et al. 1996). Falk and others looked at assigning design values to material from wood salvaged from building deconstruction projects (Falk et al. 2008, Lantz and Falk 1997). Even for newly produced lumber, a certain amount of uncertainty will always be associated with design value estimation. Assigning design values to in situ lumber and timber is more difficult because it requires judgment about the condition of members that you cannot fully access. It also requires you to judge how the prior load and environmental history has affected the member. An inspector must always be aware that judgments can only be made on what you can see and something detrimental could be lurking in the unexposed portions of the member.

11.1 Must-have documents

There are three must-have documents for someone trying to estimate a design value:

- The National Design Specification (NDS) Supplement *Design Values for Wood Construction,* which lists all currently approved design values for visually graded lumber and timber (AWC 2012)
- ASTM standard D 2555 *Standard Practice for Establishing Wood Strength Values* (ASTM 2012b)
- ASTM standard D 245 *Standard Practice for Establishing Structural Grades and Related Allowable Properties for Visually Graded Lumber* (ASTM 2012a)

The NDS Supplement can be obtained from the American Wood Council, 222 Catoctin Circle SE, Suite 201, Leesburg, VA 20175 (www.awc.org). The ASTM standards can be obtained from ASTM International, 100 Barr Harbor Drive, P.O. Box C700, West Conshohocken, PA 19428–2959 (www.ASTM.org).

11.2 Words of caution about estimating design values

Many times an inspector will not be able to see all sides of a member when trying to estimate its grade and condition. Even for very experienced certified graders, all that can truly be said about members that are observed in place is that no defects were found for the sections observed that exclude a member from a grade. There is no guarantee that this grade estimate applies to the unreachable portions of the member. The size of defects on exposed surfaces will provide some clue as to unexposed surfaces. Some confidence in a grade assignment may be gained from the grade assessment of other more accessible members. Great care, however, should be taken when determining the design values for members in place. Reducing the design value of the member by an additional uncertainty factor (Un)—perhaps as great as 2—is a reasonable thing to do.

11.3 Steps in making a first estimate of design values for members

Once you have identified the species of wood involved, determined the dimension, established the condition, and estimated a grade, follow the steps Fig. 11.1 to establish an estimate of design values for the members you have chosen. The path to assigning design values may seem confusing at first glance. Examples of each are provided to help guide the reader through the design value estimation process. Only Select Structural, No. 1, No. 2, and No. 3 grades are considered for assigning design values.

After the species, size, condition, and grade of a member is established, the next step in estimating a design value is to determine whether the species can be found in the list of species that have design values in the NDS supplement (AWC 2012). If a wood member has remained dry and does not have excessive decay, damage, splitting, or checking, one can assume that the member has equivalent properties of material produced today. A list of current species in the NDS supplement is given in Table 11.1.

Species listed in the NDS Supplement include the most common species that are present in wooden bridges. Procedures for estimating design values for species that are found in the NDS Supplement are given in Section 11.4. Note that some species listed in Table 11.1 are found as groups or individually. For example, a mixed oak group and northern red oak are both listed. If you are confident of your wood identification, use values for the individual species; otherwise it is best to use the more conservative estimate for the species group. If the species you have is not in the list of species given in Table 11.1, then you should proceed directly to Section 11.5. Your estimate of design values will depend on whether small clear wood property data for your species exist. Alternatively, you might use the low "sweeper group" design values (such as Northern Species or Western woods) and the methods of Section 11.4 for an initial estimate of design values.

Member grading examples in Table 9.6 are also used to illustrate design value assignment. Members 1, 2, 3, 4, 6, and 7 in Table 9.6 are all species listed in the NDS supplement. No design value need be calculated for Member 1 in Table 9.6 because it was identified through close inspection to have severe decay and needs to be replaced. The other five members are assigned estimated design values in Section 11.4. Members 5 and 8 in Table 9.6 are not in the NDS Supplement and are assigned estimated design values in Section 11.5. All estimated design values reported below apply the rounding rules specified in ASTM D 245 (Table 11.2).

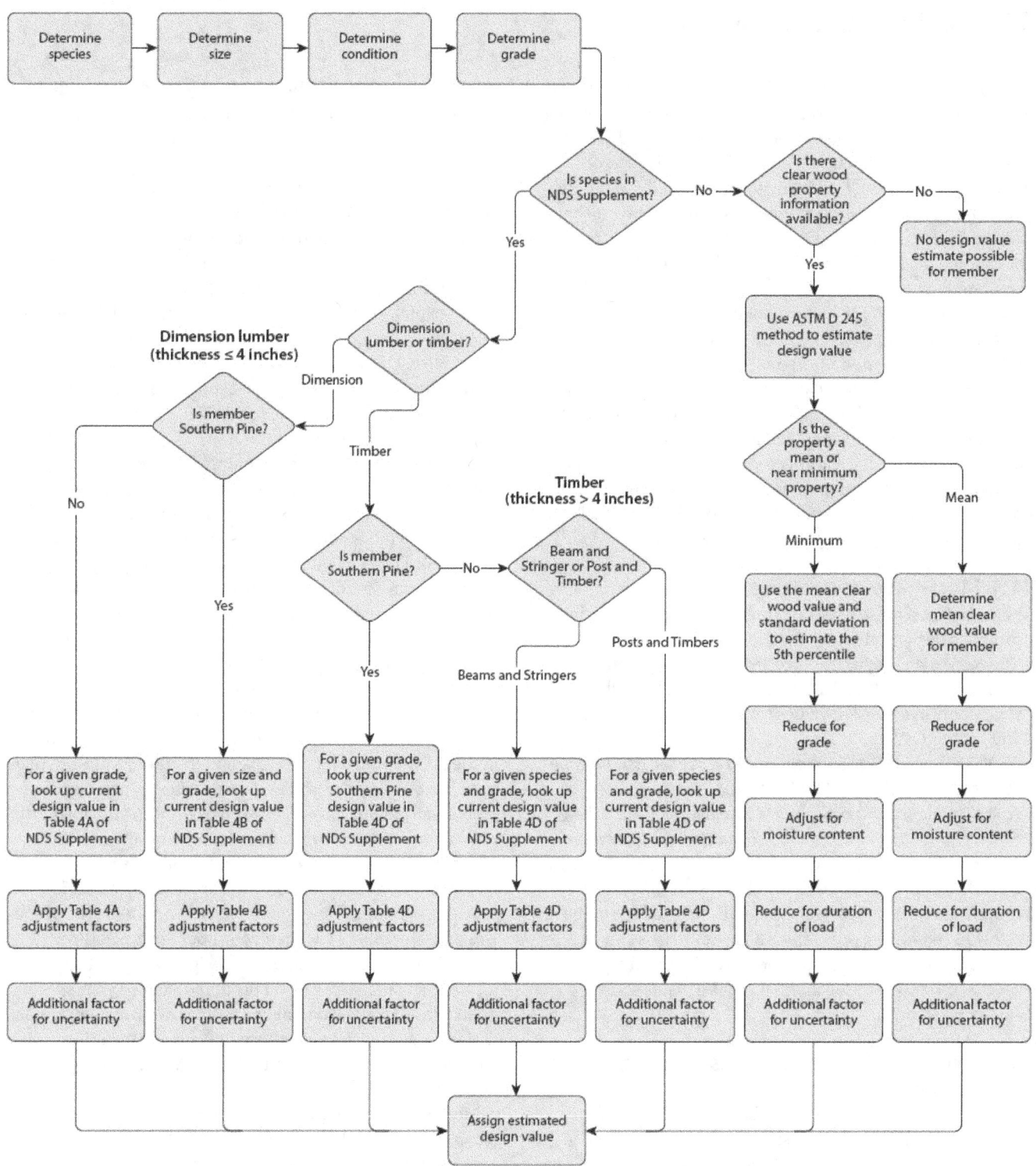

Figure 11.1—Flow chart for estimated design value assignment.

Abbreviations used in this chapter

C_f: Size factors

E: Mean modulus of elasticity

E_{min}: Lower bound of modulus of elasticity

F_b: Design value for stress in bending

F_t: Design value for stress in parallel to grain in tension

F_v: Design value for stress in horizontal shear

F_{cperp}: Design value for stress perpendicular to grain in compression

$F_{c//}$: Design value for stress parallel to the grain in tension

Un: Uncertainty factor that reflects the inspector's confidence in the observed grade or condition

Str. LF: Structural Light Framing (2–4 in. thick, 2–4 in. wide)

Str. J&P: Structural Joist and Plank (2–4 in. thick, 5 in. and wider)

B-S: Beam or Stringer (5 in. and thicker, width more than 2 in. greater than thickness)

P-T: Post or Timber (5 by 5 in. and larger, width not more than 2 in. greater than thickness)

11.4 Assigning estimated design values for species found in the NDS Supplement

If the species of the member you are interested in is in the NDS Supplement, your assignment of design values is rather straightforward. Once a grade estimate has been established, determining the design values for a member is a matter of reading the design values for that particular species from a table in the NDS supplement and applying the appropriate moisture, size, and uncertainty reduction factors.

Depending on size and grade of the member, design values for dimension lumber and timber can be found in one of three tables (4A, 4B, or 4D) in the NDS supplement. The members in Table 9.6 provide examples that use each type of table.

Visually graded structural wood products are divided into two broad use categories—dimension lumber and timbers. If the smallest dimension of the member is less than 4.5 in. thick, the material can be considered dimension lumber. If the member is 5 in. or larger in smallest dimension, it is considered a timber.

Dimension lumber properties are tabulated in two different tables depending on species. If the member is not Southern Pine, you would look up the design values in table 4A; otherwise, if the member is Southern Pine you would look up the properties in table 4B of the NDS Supplement.

For timbers, design values for all species can be found in table 4D of the NDS Supplement. Timbers, with the exception of Southern Pine timber, are further subdivided into use categories with different values for timbers that can be described as a Beam or Stringer or as Post and Timber. Southern Pine members have no distinction in design values based on use category.

11.4.1 Dimension lumber species found in NDS Supplement

Two subcategories of dimension lumber are (1) species that are not Southern Pine and (2) species that are Southern Pine. Design value estimates for each category are determined differently.

Non-Southern Pine dimension lumber species

For members that are dimension lumber size and are not Southern Pine, design values found in table 4A in the NDS Supplement apply (AWC 2012). The values in table 4A are primarily for nominal 2- by 12-in. dimension lumber. These tabulated values must be corrected to the desired size using the size factors shown in Table 11.3. Members 2, 3, and 4 in Table 9.6 fall into this category of dimension lumber. The step-by-step estimation of design values for members 2, 3, and 4 are given in Tables 11.4, 11.5, and 11.6, respectively.

Table 11.4 shows steps for calculating estimated design values for member 2. Member 2 in Table 9.6 was identified as a piece of 2 by 6 Douglas-fir dimension lumber with a grade stamp that identified the grade of the member as No. 1. It is an example of a member that fits into the dimension lumber size category (1.5 to 4 in. thick) and is not Southern Pine. The member was in good condition, and current design values for 2 by 12 No. 1 in table 4A of the NDS supplement apply. The appropriate size adjustments given in Table 11.3 are needed to convert these values to 2 by 6. Finally, because only 70% of the member was easily accessible, an additional uncertainty factor is applied as a precaution, giving the estimated design values listed in the far right column of Table 11.4. The estimated F_b value, for example, is 900 lb/in².

Table 11.5 shows estimated design values for member 3 in Table 9.6, which was identified as a northern red oak 2- by 6-in. member with an approximate grade of No. 2. This is another example of a member that fits into the dimension lumber size category (1.5- to 4-in. thick) and is not Southern Pine. There was good access to 70% of the member. The baseline design values for northern red oak can be determined from table 4A of the NDS Supplement. Once again the appropriate size factors C_f shown in Table 11.3 must be applied to convert the member to a 2 by 6 size. Finally, a similar uncertainty factor of 0.7 is applied because not all the member was visible when graded. The resulting estimated design values for member is given in the far right column of Table 11.5.

Table 11.5 shows estimated design values for member 4 in Table 9.6, which was identified as a 2- by 7.5-in. piece of cottonwood, which is closest to the current dimension of a nominal 2 by 8. The approximate grade for this member was determined to be No. 2. The baseline design values for cottonwood can be found in table 4A of the NDS supplement.

The appropriate size factors C_f shown in Table 11.3 must be applied to convert the member to a 2 by 8 size. During inspection, notes indicated that there was not good access to this member; only 50% of the member was visible on three of the four sides. This lack of access introduces a great deal of uncertainty into the estimate of grade, so a considerable reduction (Un = 0.5) in design value estimates is certainly advised. The resulting estimated design values are given in the far right column of Table 11.6.

Southern Pine dimension lumber in the NDS Supplement

Table 11.7 shows steps for determining an estimated design value for member 5. Member 5 in Table 9.6 was identified as a 2- by 4-in. Southern Pine member whose approximate grade was No. 2. The size-specific design values for Southern Pine dimension lumber are tabulated in table 4B of the NDS supplement. To estimate design values, the inspector needs to find the entry that corresponds to the grade and closest size of the member of interest. In this case, for example, the 2 by 4 No. 2 F_b given in table 4B is 1,100 lb/in². Because the values are size-specific, a size adjustment factor is not necessary. The inspection notes also indicated easy access to all sides, so an uncertainty reduction is not needed. Estimated design values listed in the far right column for member 5 is, in this case, the value given for Southern Pine 2 by 4 No. 2 of table 4B of the NDS Supplement.

11.4.2 Timber values found in NDS Supplement

The timber design values are found in table 4D of the NDS Supplement. There are again differences between how you treat Southern Pine and other species, but this time the difference is not as exaggerated. A different set of size adjustments apply to timbers than did to dimension lumber. For timbers that are subjected to loads applied to the narrow face, tabulated design values for bending are adjusted by a size adjustment found in ASTM D 245. Other properties do not receive a size adjustment. If the member depth is greater than 12 in., a new F_n can be calculated using

$$F_n = \left(\frac{12}{d}\right)^{1/9} F_o$$

where d is member depth, F_o is original bending strength, and F_n is adjusted bending strength.

Southern Pine timbers

Southern Pine timbers have no distinction between the use classes of Beams or Stringers and Post and Timbers. Therefore, you only need to find the Southern Pine timber values for the grade you are interested in and apply them to the member.

Table 11.8 shows estimated design values for member 7. Member 7 in Table 9.6 was identified as a 5.5- by 7.5-in. Southern Pine member whose observable knots and slope of grain classified the member as a No. 1 timber. Design values for Southern Pine for this size and grade can be

obtained directly from table 4D of the NDS Supplement. Inspection notes indicate that there was not good access to this member; only 50% of the member was visible on three of four sides. This suggests the need for a considerable uncertainty factor of 0.5. Estimated design values for member 7 are given in the far right column of Table 11.8.

Non-Southern Pine timbers

For non-Southern Pine members, the value in the NDS Supplement that is appropriate for the member is linked to its species, dimensions, estimated grade, and use. If the member is 5 in. thick and its width is more than 2 in. greater than thickness, the member is a Beam or Stringer. If the member is 5 by 5 in. and larger with a width not more than 2 in. greater than thickness, the member is a Post and Timber.

Table 11.9 shows estimated design values for member 8. Member 8 in Table 9.6 was identified as a 7.5- by 9.5-in. Douglas-fir member that had observable knots and slope of grain that would approximate a Select Structural piece of timber. The member size means that it can be classified as a Post and Timber. The design values for Select Structural Douglas-fir Post and Timber can be obtained in table 4D of the NDS Supplement. Inspection notes indicate that there was easy access to all sides, so no uncertainty factor is applied. Estimated design values for member 8 are given in the far right column of Table 11.9.

11.5 Assigning estimated design values for species not found in the NDS Supplement

If the species of the member is not in the NDS Supplement, design value estimates are even more uncertain. Strength and stiffness information on that species must be found. If small clear wood test values are available for the species you have identified, using the methods listed in ASTM D 245 as a guide, the equation

$$F_x = (\text{Property}) \cdot \frac{1}{\text{adjfac}} \cdot \text{Grade} \cdot \text{MC} \cdot \text{Size} \cdot \text{Un}$$

will allow for a design value estimate of F_x, which is the particular member property times an adjustment for duration of load and factor of safety (adjfac), grade (Grade), moisture content (MC), size (Size), and uncertainty (Un).

For bending, tension, shear, and compression parallel to grain design values, the estimated 5th percentile for each property is needed to estimate the design value. The 5th percentile for the species can be estimated by the (Avg – 1.645σ), where Avg is the average green small clear strength value for the small clear test result in Table 9.1 and σ is the standard deviation for the species. The standard deviation can be approximated by using the average coefficient of variation for most wood properties (given in Table 11.10) times the average clear wood strength. The species' mean clear wood modulus of elasticity (MOE) and compression perpendicular to grain (C_{perp}) stress values can be used to determine an estimate of MOE and C_{perp} design values.

The adjustment factors (adjfac) suggested in D 245 for various clear wood properties are given in Table 11.11. This factor is meant to account for duration of load and a safety factor.

The Grade adjustment is based on the assumed strength ratio for a particular visual grade. Estimated strength ratios for cross grain and density have been obtained empirically; strength ratios for other growth characteristics have been derived theoretically. Particular grades have had approximate strength ratios associated with them. The strength ratio estimates for Grade are given in Table 11.12.

The Size adjustment is based on a size adjustment factor applied to the bending clear wood value. This factor adjusts the small clear wood specimen test result obtained at a 2-in. dimension to the dimension of the member. The adjustment

$$\text{Size} = \left(\frac{2}{d}\right)^{1/9}$$

for size can be determined by using the member depth of the member d and

Finally, as in previous examples, an uncertainty factor (Un) adjustment is recommended to reflect the uncertainty associated with determining the grade and condition of the member.

Most species not in the NDS supplement but used in covered bridges can be found in Table 9.1. Two examples from Table 9.6, dimension lumber member 6 and timber member 9, are given below. Other example calculations of design values using clear wood information can be found in Bendtsen and Galligan (1978).

11.5.1 Member is dimension lumber size
Table 11.13 shows steps for estimating design values for member 6. Member 6 of Table 9.6 was identified as a 2- by 6-in. American chestnut Structural Joist and Plank that had observable defects and a slope of grain that classified it as a No. 2 piece of dimension lumber. The average clear wood mean values for American chestnut from Table 9.1, which have been converted to pounds per square inch, are in column 1. Where applicable, these values are adjusted to a 5th percentile estimate in column 2. The hardwood adjustment factors from Table 11.10 and the estimated grade strength ratio from Table 11.11 are in columns 3 and 4, respectively. Moisture adjustment factors for American chestnut from green to dry are available in table X1.1 of ASTM D 2555 and are listed in column 5. Only the bending stress value is adjusted for size in column 6. Inspection notes indicate that there was quite good access, resulting in an uncertainty factor of 0.8. The estimated design values for member 6 are given in far right column.

11.5.2 Member is timber size
Table 11.14 shows steps for estimating design values for member 9. Member 9 of Table 9.6 was identified as a 5- by

8-in. ash beam and stringer that had observable defects approximating a No. 2 grade timber. The average clear wood mean values for white ash from Table 9.1, which have been converted to pounds per square inch, are tabulated in column 1. Where applicable, these values are adjusted to a 5th percentile estimate in column 2. The hardwood adjustment factors from Table 11.10 and the estimated grade strength ratio from Table 11.11 are in columns 3 and 4, respectively. Moisture adjustment factors for white ash from green to dry are available in table X1.1 of ASTM D 2555 and are listed in column 5. Only the bending stress value is adjusted for size in column 6. Inspection notes indicate that only 70% of the member was accessible, so an uncertainty factor of 0.7 is applied to the estimate. Estimated design values for member 9 are given in far right column.

11.6 Final words of advice for design value estimation
This manual is meant to provide the reader with basic information about design value assignment to wooden bridge members. It gives the inspector a basic method for estimating design value for members. The most accurate estimate of the in-place design value for a member would be obtained by employing a certified grader with extensive experience and knowledge of the various structural lumber grades. The field inspector, however, should be able to get a good sense of the quality of the members that are in the structure and determine if current members are in the "ball park" of capacity needed.

An inspector will often not be able to see a large portion of a member, and judgment will be required based on the quality of wood in members that are visible in accessible areas. Confidence in the condition of members also plays a big role. Keep good records indicating the amount of the member that was accessible and your confidence of the estimated grade. Design values for the member may require an adjustment based on your confidence in your determined grade. The uncertainty factor that has been applied in the example estimations is one such adjustment.

Decisions made by the inspector on the condition of a wooden bridge, based on the inspector's analysis of calculations or technical data, are ultimately the responsibility of the inspector. Understanding the basis of the information or data upon which they rely is the primary responsibility of the inspector. This field guide is based on publicly available information. Some of that information comes from grading rules published by various trade associations or grades identified within the *National Design Specification for Wood Construction*. The Federal Highway Administration and the USDA Forest Service, while providing financial and administrative support, are not responsible for the content or use of the information by individuals. Be aware that changes in grading rules occasionally take place, and the inspector is responsible for confirming what the current rules are.

Table 11.1—Species with design values in the NDS Supplement (AWC 2012)

NDS species or species combination	Species included in combination	Table with design value
Alaska Cedar		4A
Alaska Hemlock		4A
Alaska Spruce	Alaska Sitka Spruce Alaska White Spruce	4A
Alaska Yellow Cedar		4A
Aspen	Big Tooth Aspen Quaking Aspen	4A
Baldcypress		4A, 4D
Balsam Fir		4D
Beech-Birch-Hickory	American Beech Bitternut Hickory Mockernut Hickory Nutmeg Hickory Pecan Hickory Pignut Hickory Shagbark Hickory Shellbark Hickory Sweet Birch Water Hickory Yellow Birch	4A, 4D
Coast Sitka Spruce		4A, 4D, 4E
Douglas Fir-Larch	Douglas-fir Western Larch	4A, 4C, 4D, 4E
Douglas Fir-Larch (North)	Douglas-fir Western Larch	4A, 4C, 4D, 4E
Douglas Fir-South		4A, 4C, 4D, 4E
Eastern Hemlock		4D
Eastern Hemlock-Balsam Fir	Balsam Fir Eastern Hemlock Tamarack	4A
Eastern Hemlock-Tamarack	Eastern Hemlock Tamarack	4A, 4D, 4E
Eastern Hemlock-Tamarack (North)	Eastern Hemlock Tamarack	4D, 4E
Eastern Softwoods	Balsam Fir Black Spruce Eastern Hemlock Eastern White Pine Jack Pine Norway (Red) Pine Pitch Pine Red Spruce Tamarack White Spruce	4A

Table 11.1—Species with design values in the NDS Supplement (AWC 2012)—con.

NDS species or species combination	Species included in combination	Table with design value
Eastern Spruce	Black Spruce Red Spruce White Spruce	4D, 4E
Eastern White Pine		4A, 4D, 4E
Eastern White Pine (North)		4E
Hem-Fir	California Red Fir Grand Fir Noble Fir Pacific Silver Fir Western Hemlock White Fir	4A, 4C, 4D, 4E
Hem-Fir (North)	Amabilis Fir Western Hemlock	4A, 4C, 4D, 4E
Mixed Maple	Black Maple Red Maple Silver Maple Sugar Maple	4A, 4D
Mixed Oak	All Oak species under NeLMA rules	4A, 4D
Mixed Southern Pine	Any species in the Southern Pine species combination, plus either or both of the following: Pond Pine, Virginia Pine	4B, 4C, 4D
Mountain Hemlock		4D
Northern Pine	Jack Pine Norway (Red) Pine Pitch Pine	4D, 4E
Northern Red Oak	Black Oak Northern Red Oak Pin Oak Scarlet Oak	4A, 4D
Northern Species	Any species graded under NLGA rules except Red Alder, White Birch, and Norway Spruce	4A, 4D, 4E
Northern White Cedar		4A, 4D, 4E
Ponderosa Pine		4D, 4E
Red Maple		4A, 4D
Red Oak	Black Oak Cherrybark Oak Laurel Oak Northern Red Oak Pin Oak Scarlet Oak Southern Red Oak Water Oak Willow Oak	4A, 4D
Red Pine		4D, 4E
Redwood		4A, 4D, 4E
Sitka Spruce		4D, 4E

Table 11.1—Species with design values in the NDS Supplement (AWC 2012)—con.

NDS species or species combination	Species included in combination	Table with design value
Southern Pine	Loblolly Pine Longleaf Pine Shortleaf Pine Slash Pine	4A, 4C, 4D, 4E
Spruce-Pine-Fir	Alpine Fir Balsam Fir Black Spruce Engelmann Spruce Jack Pine Lodgepole Pine Red Spruce White Spruce	4A, 4C, 4D, 4E
Spruce-Pine-Fir (South)	Balsam Fir Black Spruce Engelmann Spruce Jack Pine Lodgepole Pine Norway (Red) Pine Red Spruce Sitka Spruce White Spruce	4A, 4C, 4D, 4E
Western Cedars	Alaska Cedar Incense Cedar Port Orford Cedar Western Red Cedar	4A, 4C, 4D, 4E
Western Cedars (North)	Pacific Coast Yellow Cedar Western Red Cedar	4A, 4C, 4D, 4E
Western Hemlock		4A, 4C, 4D, 4E
Western Hemlock (North)		4A, 4C, 4D, 4E
Western White Pine		4A, 4C, 4D, 4E
Western Woods	Any species in the Douglas Fir-Larch, Douglas Fir-South, Hem-Fir, and Spruce-Pine-Fir (South) species combinations, plus any or all of the following: Alpine Fir, Idaho White Pine, Mountain Hemlock, Ponderosa Pine, Sugar Pine	4A, 4C, 4D, 4E
White Oak	Bur Oak Chestnut Oak Live Oak Overcup Oak Post Oak Swamp Chestnut Oak Swamp White Oak White Oak	
Yellow Cedar		4A
Yellow Poplar		4A

Table 4A: Reference Design Values for Visually Graded Dimension Lumber (2–4 in. thick).

Table 4B: Reference Design Values for Visually Graded Southern Pine Dimension Lumber (2–4 in. thick).

Table 4C: Reference Design Values for Mechanically Graded Dimension Lumber.

Table 4D: Reference Design Values for Visually Graded timbers (5 by 5 in. and larger).

Table 4E: Reference Design Values for Visually Graded Decking.

Table 11.2—Rounding Rules (ASTM D 245-11)

Bending, tension parallel, and compression parallel to grain	For design value stresses 1,000 lb/in² (6.9 MPa) or greater, round to nearest 50 lb/in² (340 kPa)
	For design value stresses less than 1,000 lb/in² (6.9 MPa), round to nearest 25 lb/in² (170 kPa)
Horizontal shear and compression perpendicular to grain	Round to nearest 5 lb/in² (34 kPa)
Modulus of elasticity	Round to nearest 100,000 lb/in² (69 GPa)

Table 11.3—Size factors, C_f

Grades	Width (in.)	F_b		F_t	$F_{c//}$
		Thickness			
		2 and 3 in.	4 in.		
Select Structural, No. 1, No. 2, and No. 3	2 and 3	1.5	1.5	1.5	1.15
	5	1.4	1.4	1.4	1.1
	6	1.3	1.3	1.3	1.1
	8	1.2	1.3	1.2	1.05
	10	1.1	1.2	1.1	1.0
	12	1.0	1.1	1.0	1.0
	14	0.9	1.0	0.9	0.9

Table 11.4—Example of design value estimation for No. 1 Douglas-fir 2 by 6

Species	Estimated member size	Estimated member grade	Purpose	Property	Table 4A baseline design value	C_f Size adjustment factor	Un[a]	Estimated design value
Douglas-fir	1.5 by 5.5 in.	No. 1	Str. J&P	F_b (lb/in²)	1,000	1.3	0.7	900
				F_t (lb/in²)	675	1.3	0.7	600
				F_v (lb/in²)	180	1.0	0.7	125
				F_{cperp} (lb/in²)	625	1.0	0.7	440
				$F_{c//}$ (lb/in²)	1,500	1.1	0.7	1,150
				E (10^6 lb/in²)	1,700,000	1.0	0.7	1,200,000
				E_{min} (10^6 lb/in²)	620,000	1.0	0.7	400,000

[a]Un, uncertainty.

Table 11.5—Example of design value estimation for No. 2 Northern Red Oak 2 by 6

Species	Estimated member size	Estimated member grade	Purpose	Property	Table 4A baseline design value	C_f Size adjustment factor	Un[a]	Estimated design value
Northern Red Oak	2 by 6	No. 2	Str. J&P	F_b (lb/in²)	975	1.3	0.7	890
				F_t (lb/in²)	575	1.3	0.7	525
				F_v (lb/in²)	220	1.0	0.7	155
				F_{cperp} (lb/in²)	885	1.0	0.7	620
				$F_{c//}$ (lb/in²)	725	1.1	0.7	560
				E (10^6 lb/in²)	1,300,000	1.0	0.7	910,000
				E_{min} (10^6 lb/in²)	470,000	1.0	0.7	329,000

[a]Un, uncertainty.

Table 11.6—Example of design value estimation for No. 2 Cottonwood 2 by 8

Species	Estimated member size	Estimated member grade	Purpose	Property	Table 4A baseline design value	C_f Size adjustment factor	Un[a]	Estimated design value
Cottonwood	2 by 8	No. 2	Str. J&P	F_b (lb/in²)	625	1.2	0.5	375
				F_t (lb/in²)	350	1.2	0.5	210
				F_v (lb/in²)	125	1	0.5	65
				F_{cperp} (lb/in²)	320	1	0.5	160
				$F_{c//}$ (lb/in²)	475	1.05	0.5	250
				E (10^6 lb/in²)	1,100,000	1	0.5	550,000
				E_{min} (10^6 lb/in²)	400,000	1	0.5	200,000

[a]Un, uncertainty.

Table 11.7—Example of design value estimation for No. 2 Southern Pine 2 by 4

Species	Estimated member size	Estimated member grade	Purpose	Property	Table 4B baseline design value	C_f Size adjustment factor	Un[a]	Estimated design value
Southern Pine	2 by 4	No. 2	Str. LF	F_b (lb/in^2)	1,100	1	1.0	1,100
				F_t (lb/in^2)	675	1	1.0	675
				F_v (lb/in^2)	175	1	1.0	175
				F_{cperp} (lb/in^2)	565	1	1.0	565
				$F_{c//}$ (lb/in^2)	1,450	1	1.0	1,450
				E (10^6 lb/in^2)	1,400,000	1	1.0	1,400,000
				E_{min} (10^6 lb/in^2)	510,000	1	1.0	510,000

[a]Un, uncertainty.

Table 11.8—Example of design value estimation for No. 1 Southern Pine 6 by 8

Species	Estimated member size	Estimated member grade	Purpose	Property	Table 4D baseline design value	C_f Size adjustment factor	Un[a]	Estimated design value
Southern Pine	6 by 8	No. 1	P-T	F_b (lb/in^2)	1,350	1	0.5	675
				F_t (lb/in^2)	900	1	0.5	450
				F_v (lb/in^2)	165	1	0.5	85
				F_{cperp} (lb/in^2)	375	1	0.5	190
				$F_{c//}$ (lb/in^2)	825	1	0.5	415
				E (10^6 lb/in^2)	1,500,000	1	0.5	750,000
				E_{min} (10^6 lb/in^2)	550,000	1	0.5	275,000

[a]Un, uncertainty.

Table 11.9—Example of design value estimation for Select Structural Douglas-fir 8 by 10

Species	Estimated member size	Estimated member grade	Purpose	Property	Table 4D baseline design value	C_f Size adjustment factor	Un[a]	Estimated design value
Douglas-fir	8 by 10	Sel. Str.	P-T	F_b (lb/in²)	1,500	1	1.0	1,500
				F_t (lb/in²)	1,000	1	1.0	1,000
				F_v (lb/in²)	170	1	1.0	170
				F_{cperp} (lb/in²)	625	1	1.0	625
				$F_{c//}$ (lb/in²)	1,150	1	1.0	1,150
				E (10^6 lb/in²)	1,600,000	1	1.0	1,600,000
				E_{min} (10^6 lb/in²)	580,000	1	1.0	580,000

[a]Un, uncertainty.

Table 11.10—Average coefficient of variation for clear wood properties (FPL 2010)

	Bending	Modulus of elasticity	Tensile strength parallel to grain	Compressive strength parallel to grain	Horizontal shear strength	Proportional limit stress at deformation in compression perpendicular to grain
Coefficient of variation	16	22	25	18	14	28

Table 11.11—Adjustment factors to be applied to the clear wood properties (ASTM D 245-11)

	Bending	Modulus of elasticity	Tensile strength parallel to grain	Compressive strength parallel to grain	Horizontal shear strength	Proportional limit stress at deformation in compression perpendicular to grain
Softwoods	2.1	0.94	2.1	1.9	2.1	1.67
Hardwoods	2.3	0.94	2.3	2.1	2.3	1.67

Table 11.12—Assumed strength ratio values for rough estimate of design values (Bendtsen and Galligan 1978)

Grades	Assumed strength ratio					
	Bending	Tension	Shear	C_{perp}	Compression	MOE
Clear wood	100	100	100	100	100	100
Select Structural	65	65*55	50	100	69	100
No. 1	55	55*55	50	100	62	100
No. 2	45	45*55	50	100	52	90
No. 3	26	26*55	50	100	33	80

Table 11.13—Example of design value estimation for No. 2 American Chestnut 2 by 6

Species	Estimated member size	Estimated member grade	Purpose	Property	Clear wood mean (lb/in²)	5th Pctl. Est.	adjfac[a]	Grade	MC	Size	Un[b]	Estimated design value (lb/in²)
American Chestnut	2 by 6	Sel. Str.	Str. J&P	F_b (lb/in²)	5,655	4,170	2.3	0.45	1.53	0.894	0.8	900
				F_t (lb/in²)	5,655	3,330	2.3	0.247	1.53	1	0.8	450
				F_v (lb/in²)	800	615	2.3	0.5	1.36	1	0.8	145
				F_{cperp} (lb/in²)	305	N/A	1.67	1	2.00	1	0.8	290
				$F_{c//}$ (lb/in²)	2,465	1,735	2.1	0.50	2.15	1	0.8	650
				E (10^6 lb/in²)	930,000	N/A	0.94	0.9	1.32	1	0.8	900,000

[a]adjfac, adjustment factor.
[b]Un, uncertainty.

Table 11.14—Example of design value estimation for No. 2 White Ash 5 by 8

Species	Estimated member size	Estimated member grade	Purpose	Property	Clear wood mean (lb/in²)	5th Pctl. Est.	adjfac[a]	Grade	MC	Size	Un[b]	Estimated design value (lb/in²)
White Ash	5 by 8	No. 2	B-S	F_b (lb/in²)	9,570	7,055	2.3	0.45	1.57	0.857	0.7	1,500
				F_t (lb/in²)	5,265	5,635	2.3	0.247	1.57	1	0.7	650
				F_v (lb/in²)	1,350	1,040	2.3	0.5	1.41	1	0.7	225
				F_{cperp} (lb/in²)	665	N/A	1.67	1	1.73	1	0.7	385
				$F_{c//}$ (lb/in²)	3,990	2,805	2.1	0.50	1.86	1	0.7	975
				E (10^6 lb/in²)	1,435,000	N/A	0.94	0.9	1.21	1	0.7	1,200,000

[a]adjfac, adjustment factor.
[b]Un, uncertainty.

References

ANSI/AWC NDS. American Wood Council, National Design Specification for Wood Construction [Current Edition]. Leesburg, VA: American Wood Council.

ASTM. 1907. Proceedings of the tenth annual meeting held at Atlantic City, New Jersey, June 20, 21, 22, 1907. Vol. VII. Philadelphia, PA: American Society for Testing Materials.

ASTM. 1908. Proceedings of the eleventh annual meeting held at Atlantic City, New Jersey, June 23–27, 1908. Vol. VIII. Philadelphia, PA: American Society for Testing Materials.

ASTM. 2013. Annual book of standards, Vol. 04.10. West Conshohocken, PA: American Society for Testing and Materials.

ASTM D 245–06. Standard methods for establishing structural grades for visually graded lumber.

ASTM D 2555–06. Standard methods for establishing clear wood strength values.

ASTM D 4444–08. Standard test method for laboratory standardization and calibration of hand-held moisture meters.

Anthony & Associates. 2009. A grading protocol for structural lumber and timber. Submitted to: Association for Preservation Technology International, Springfield, IL, and National Center for Preservation Technology and Training, Natchitoches, LA. National Center for Preservation Technology and Training Grant No. MT-2210-05-NC-05; May. 45 p.

Anthony, R.W. 2007. Basics of wood inspection: Considerations for historic preservation. APT Bulletin. 38(2–3): 1–6.

Anthony, R.W.; Dugan, K.D.; Anthony, D.J. 2009. A grading protocol for structural lumber and timber in historic structures. APT Bulletin. 40(2): 3–9.

AWC. 2011. National Design Specification (NDS) supplement: design values for wood construction 2012 edition. Leesburg, VA: American Wood Council.

Bendtsen, B.A.; Galligan, W.L. 1978. Deriving allowable properties of lumber (A practical guide for interpretation of ASTM standards). Gen. Tech. Rep. FPL–GTR–20. Madison WI: U.S. Department of Agriculture, Forest Service, Forest Products Laboratory. 31 p.

Brashaw, B.K.; Vatalaro, R.J.; Wacker, J.P.; Ross, R.J. 2005a. Condition assessment of timber bridges: 1. evaluation of a micro-drilling resistance tool. Gen. Tech. Rep.

FPL–GTR–159. Madison, WI: U.S. Department of Agriculture, Forest Service, Forest Products Laboratory. 8 p.

Brashaw, B.K.; Vatalaro, R.J.; Wacker, J.P.; Ross, R.J. 2005b. Condition assessment of timber bridges: 2. Evaluation of several stress-wave tools. Gen. Tech. Rep. FPL–GTR–160. Madison, WI: U.S. Department of Agriculture, Forest Service, Forest Products Laboratory. 11 p.

DOC. [Current edition]. American softwood lumber standard. Voluntary product standard PS–20. Washington, D.C.: U.S. Department of Commerce.

Green, D.W.; Evans, J.W. 2001. Evolution of standardized procedures for adjusting lumber properties for change in moisture content. Gen. Tech. Rep. FPL–GTR–127. Madison, WI: U.S. Department of Agriculture, Forest Service, Forest Products Laboratory.

Falk, R.H.; Maul, D.G.; Cramer, S.M.; Evans, J.; Herian, V. 2008. Engineering properties of Douglas-fir lumber reclaimed from deconstructed buildings. Res. Pap. FPL–RP–650. Madison, WI: U.S. Department of Agriculture, Forest Service, Forest Products Laboratory. 47 p.

FPL. 2010. Wood handbook—wood as an engineering material. Gen. Tech. Rep. FPL–GTR–190. Madison, WI: U.S. Department of Agriculture, Forest Service, Forest Products Laboratory. 508 p.

Gonzalez, J.M.; Morrell, J.J. 2012. Effects of environmental factors on decay rates of selected white- and brown-rot fungi. Wood and Fiber Science. 44(4): 343–356.

Ivory, E.P.; White, D.G.; Upson, A.T. 1923. Standard grading specifications for yard lumber. Circular 296. Washington, DC: U.S. Department of Agriculture. 75 p.

Kukay, B.; White, R.; Todd, C.; Jahn, T. 2013. Evaluating fire-damaged components of timber bridges and structures. Structures Congress 2013: 758–767. doi: 10.1061/9780784412848.067

Lantz, S.F.; Falk, R.H. 1997. Feasibility of recycling timber from military industrial buildings. In: The use of recycled wood and paper in building applications. Proceedings 7286. Madison, WI: Forest Products Society: 41–48.

Loferski, J.R.; Dolan, J.D.; Lang E. 1996. Determining mechanical properties by nondestructive evaluation and testing methods in wood buildings. In: Kelley, S.J., ed. Standards for preservation and rehabilitation.

West Conshohocken, PA.: American Society for Testing and Materials: 175–185.

Newlin, J.A.; Johnson, R.P.S. 1923. Basic grading rules and working stresses for structural timbers. Circular 295. Washington, DC: U.S. Department of Agriculture.

Pfaff, F.; Garrahan, P. 1984. Temperature correlation factors and combined temperature-species correction factors for the resistance type moisture meter. Project. 03–40–10–001 (unpublished). Forintek Canada Corporation, Eastern Lab.

Rinn, F. 2013. Practical application of micro-resistance drilling for timber inspection. Holztechnologie. 54 (4): 32–38.

Ross, R.J.; Pellerin, R.F.; Volny, N.; Salsig, W.W.; Falk, R.H. 1999. Inspection of timber bridges using stress wave timing nondestructive evaluation tools—A guide for use and interpretation. Gen. Tech. Rep. FPL–GTR–114. Madison, WI: U.S. Department of Agriculture, Forest Service, Forest Products Laboratory. 15 p.

Ross, R.J.; Brashaw, B.K.; Wang, X.; White, R.H.; Pellerin, R.F. 2004. Wood and timber condition assessment manual. Madison, WI: Forest Products Society. 74 p.

Smith, L.W., Wood, L.W. 1964. History of yard lumber size standards. Madison, WI.: U.S. Department of Agriculture, Forest Service, Forest Products Laboratory.

SPIB. 2002. Standard grading rules for southern pine lumber. Pensacola, FL: Southern Pine Inspection Bureau.

Wood, L.W. 1954. Structural values in old lumber. Southern Lumberman. No. 189, Dec. 15, part 2.

WWPA. 2005. Western lumber grading rules. Portland, OR: Western Wood Products Association.

www.ingramcontent.com/pod-product-compliance
Lightning Source LLC
Chambersburg PA
CBHW080314290526
45790CB00005B/2039